FROM ADHD TO A'S:

IMPROVE READING, MEMORY, AND LEARNING *QUICKLY* FOR KINESTHETIC LEARNERS

Ricki Linksman

From ADHD to A's

ISBN No: 978-1-928997-38-2

Praise for Ricki Linksman's Books and Brain-Based Learning Methods

"My child has made tremendous gains in a short time. His self-esteem has risen dramatically."

-A.P, Parent, Naperville

"My 10th grade son went from grades of 'F's" and 'D's' to 'A's' in 4 weeks. His study skills, comprehension, and memory has improved tremendously."

-Parent, Westmont

"In 6 months, my 4th grade child, who was reading 3 years below level, came up to grade level and is doing well in school."

-Parent, Lisle

"I have learned so much about how to help my son and about learning styles in general. I have to say that the frustration level when doing homework or reading has gone down dramatically.

-M.H., Chicago

"We have seen improved results in my son's tests and overall academics. In fact, he made the honor roll!! I appreciate the fact she is able to see how he best comprehends his reading material and incorporates the best plan for him. We are very happy to see his overall comprehension improve and especially his confidence. Thank you Ricki!"

-L.Z., parent

"My kindergartener is now reading 3rd grade books, and doing addition, subtraction, multiplication, and division over several months' time."

-Mr. R.M., Parent, Naperville

"For the first time, my 2nd grader could read on his grade level, and his self-esteem has increased tremendously."

-Parent, Chicago

"We wanted our 4-year-old child to qualify for a gifted school but she didn't achieve the necessary score on her first test. Within less than a year, she not only learned to read at a 3rd grade level, but was able to qualify for the gifted school. We are so thrilled with the results."

-S.D., Parent, Wheaton

"I home school my children and I learned how to accelerate their reading at home."

-Parent, Batavia

"My gifted child loves the challenging activities."

-Parent, Downers Grove

"I've looked for years for help for my son and Ricki Linksman is the only person that came through. My son has made more progress in these last 8 months than he has K through 6th grade. She provides concrete solutions to his specific areas that he needs help in. I recommend Ricki's book to anyone whose child is struggling at school or who wants to give their child an advantage to succeed. Ricki has not only helped my son to learn but his attitude and confidence has increased dramatically. I have seen amazing results for my son. Not only has his reading level improved dramatically but his confidence and enthusiasm are through the roof!"

From ADHD to A's

-S.S, Parent, Illinois

"If you are reading this, you are probably concerned about the progress your child or grandchild is making in learning to read. I was in the same position several years ago. My grandson wasn't learning to read in his school. He had been left back in the same grade twice because he could not read. He was diagnosed with ADD and a learning disability. We spent years trying to find out why he could not read because he was a bright boy. As a concerned parent or grandparent, I got on the Internet and found Ricki Linksman's National Reading Diagnostics Institute and its Keys to Reading Success® and its Superlinks to Accelerated Learning™ programs which determined what his learning style and brain hemispheric preference was. The assessment determined he was a kinesthetic and tactile learner with a right-brain hemispheric preference. It gave us a prescriptive plan to solve the problem and lessons in his best learning style. Within the first lesson of Keys to Reading Success®, using kinesthetic right-brain learning techniques, my grandson read for the first time in his life, to his joy and excitement. **After only one session with the Keys to Reading Success® materials, I watched this little guy read solid first-grade material that he had never been able to read before for the first time in his life.** Yet, several hours before that first session, he had not even known the letters of the alphabet. I almost fell out of my chair, I was so excited. I knew then that I was on the right track, and I had found the right person and right techniques and program to teach this young lad how to read. He has been reading ever since. **Within a few months, he was able to read at his grade level, and we were able to take him off his ADD medication.** We now know what works for him and we attributed it to National Reading Diagnostics Institute and Keys to

Reading Success. **The developer of Keys to Reading Success®, Ricki Linksman, is truly the Michael Jordan of reading."**

> **-Rusty Acree, Concerned Grandparent, Retd. Naval Officer, and Field Judge for University Football Games, Richmond, Virginia:**
> **-And from his grandson, who wrote:** When asked about what he liked best about his trip to Chicago, the lad wrote: "Learning to read. Thank you Mrs. Linksman."

"My daughter struggled with reading in early elementary school, and I realized that when she read to me, she was only memorizing the book and could not read on her own. Ricki Linksman at National Reading Diagnostics Institute gave the Superlinks test and found out she was a kinesthetic right brain learner and the techniques in her school were not matching how she best learned. By using kinesthetic right brain techniques for her learning. Ricki not only taught her to read at grade level within a few months, but raised her several years above her age as well. Throughout the rest of her school career, she became a top reader and student in her class, no longer needed tutoring, and ended up in honors classes. In high school, she was number eleven in overall standing in her school. She returned to National Reading Diagnostics Institute to work with Ricki Linksman for ACT test prep, in her kinesthetic right brain learning style, and got a perfect score on the English ACT! She not only gained admission to numerous universities, but she was offered several scholarships, won academic awards, and ended up selecting a college, whose scholarship is paying $25,000.00 a year for each of the four years for her tuition. We are so glad we found National Reading Diagnostics Institute and Ricki Linksman and recommend her to any parent who wants to lay the foundation early for their child's future success in high school, college, and in life."

-J.O., Parent, Wheaton, Illinois

"Our teenager did not score well on the practice test for a high school entrance exam to Benet Academy, a college preparatory school. After a few months of work at National Reading Diagnostics Institute, areas of need were targeted and our teen got 99% on the actual entrance exam and was admitted to the preparatory school."

-Parent, Lisle

"Our son was in special education classes since 1st grade and by 7th grade still had not learned to read. We brought him to Ricki Linksman for a reading diagnosis and she gave him a Keys to Reading Success® reading diagnostic test, Superlinks™ learning style and brain style test, and tutoring instruction. Our son learned to read in months and no longer needed to be in special education. His self-esteem has gone up and he is so happy now."

-B. Burke., Parent, Miami, Florida

"My high school sophomore never dropped below A's or B's before, so when he dropped to a C in English, we were beside ourselves with frustration. After using these strategies for only 6 weeks, he not only went back up to A, but was the only student in the class to receive a writing award!"

-M.H., Parent

"We did not feel our middle school son had the skills to be ready for high school. He was struggling in many of his school subjects and even needed audios to read his assigned books to him. After only two months using these strategies, he can now read by himself, and his grades have improved to the point where the principal and teachers are astounded by his amazing progress! He feels proud of himself, enjoys school now, and has boosted his vocabulary, memory, study skills, and test-taking skills. The best part is that he does not need to be read to, but can read at and above his grade level all by himself!

-K.A, Parent

From "Woman News," New York, New York:

"There is a way to learn anything you want rapidly and successfully. The technique can be applied to any sort of learning in any field you choose. Each of us has a Superlink—the easiest method for us to fully learn information. Once you've found your Superlink, you can use it to learn in ways that are easy, effortless, and automatic." —published in an article in New York's "Woman News" called, "Mind Power: Smarten Up! Tap into Your Brain's Superlink—Learning Becomes Easy, Effortless, and Automatic"

From "L.A. Parent" and "San Diego Parent," California:

"All children in California will be reading at grade level or above by the end of third grade.' With this promise, California state leaders have made reading instruction in the early grades (K through Grade 3) a top priority in the public schools. So while the politicians are trying to do their part, how can parents help their little readers measure up? According to Ricki Linksman, author of *Your Child Can Be a Great Reader*, parents should first figure out their child's learning style. "Research shows that each of us receives information in different ways. Visual learners learn best through their eyes, auditory learners through their ears, tactile learners by touching, and kinesthetic learners by moving around."

--from an article in the "L.A. Times" and "San Diego Times," called "What is Your Child's Reading Style? If You Know How Your Child Reads You Can Help Him/Her Learn," by Judy Molland

From a Public School District Superintendent:

"Ricki Linksman has synthesized the educational research into concepts which makes learning accessible to anyone. While the term differentiation of instruction is very popular in the world of education, Ricki Linksman provides concrete examples and techniques of combining learning styles with brain hemispheric preference to create an individualized "superlink." These techniques are personalized to open the pathways for anyone to learn anything quickly. For example, our junior high school went from 2/3 of the students below state level on state reading assessment tests to 2/3 of the students above state level in reading within eight months."

-Dr. Michael Early, Public School District Superintendent, Illinois, and former School Principal in West Suburban Chicago

From a Head Football Coach:

"Using these accelerated learning techniques such as teaching through learning styles has helped our university football team have its first winning season ever. The athletes learned the plays faster and better through these techniques. We also had our best academic year ever, for our academic support to our athletes."

-Ken Karcher, University Head Football Coach

From the Iowa "Gazette," Cedar Rapids, Iowa:

"Author Ricki Linksman has plenty of tips for parents who want to be sure their kids love to read, and can read well."

From Learning Identify, South Africa:

"Ricki Linksman has a heart to make a difference in the lives of those who struggle with reading. She has developed a unique learning and reading program based on brain processing and learning styles, which undertakes to teach ANYONE how to read and learn and most importantly how to comprehend the content matter. We have had remarkable success with 100's of students utilizing Ricki's Keys to Reading Success and Superlinks to Accelerated Learning program, and consider it an honor to be a part of her work." -Trish Gatland, Learning Identity, South Africa

Other Books and Resources by the Author, Ricki Linksman

(Books, eBooks, and Software about the Brain; Memory Improvement; Accelerated Learning through Learning Styles and Brain Styles; Kinesthetic, Tactile, Visual, Auditory Left and Right Brain Learners; Reading and Listening Comprehension Strategies; Accelerated Phonics; Vocabulary; Test-taking, Note-taking, and Study Skills and Test Prep for High School and College Entrance Exams, (ACT, SAT); Self-Esteem; Motivation; Concentration; and Focus
by Ricki Linksman)

How to Learn Anything Quickly: Quick, Easy Tips to Improve Memory, Reading Comprehension, Test-Taking Skills, and Learning through the Brain's Fastest Superlinks Learning Style

How to Improve Memory Quickly: Quick, Easy Tips to Improve Memory through the Brain's Fastest Superlinks Learning Style

The Fine Line between ADHD and Kinesthetic Learners: 197 Kinesthetic Activities to Quickly Improve Reading, Memory, and Learning in Just 10 Weeks: The Ultimate Parent Guide to ADD, ADHD, and Kinesthetic Learners

How to Improve Reading Comprehension Quickly by Knowing Your Personal Reading Comprehension Style: Quick, Easy Tips to Improve Comprehension through the Brain's Fastest Superlinks Learning Style

Solving Your Child's Reading Problem

From ADHD to A's: Improve Reading, Memory, and Learning Quickly for Kinesthetic Learners

Your Child Can Be a Great Reader

Keys to Reading Success™: Internet Reading Program (includes Linksman Passage Reading Tests, Linksman Phonics Diagnostic Test, and Superlinks Assessment, plus 1000s of pages of reading lesson plans in all learning styles:
Kinesthetic, Tactile, Visual, and Auditory with adaptations for right and left brain learners in reading comprehension, phonics, vocabulary, test-taking strategies, test prep, and study skills.

Superlinks to Accelerated Learning Assessment™ (includes Linksman Learning Style Preference Assessment™ and Linksman Brain Hemispheric Preference Assessment™)

Off the Wall Phonics (Accelerated K-12, College, and Adult Phonics Program to Improve Reading Comprehension, Word Reading and Fluency for Kinesthetic, Tactile, Visual, and Auditory Learners, both Right-Brain and Left-Brain Learners)

Kinesthetic Vocabulary Activities Your Child Will Love

Tactile Vocabulary Activities Your Child Will Love

How to Quickly Improve Memory and Learning for Kinesthetic Left and Right Brain Superlinks Learning Styles

How to Quickly Improve Memory and Learning for Tactile Left and Right Brain Superlinks Learning Styles

How to Quickly Improve Study, Note-taking and Test-taking Skills for Auditory Left and Right Brain Superlinks Learning Styles

Vowel and Consonant Guide

Superlinks to Accelerated Learning: Phonics Diagnostic Test

For other products, books, eBooks, software, trainings, and e-courses visit: www.readinginstruction.com
www.keyslearning.com
www.superlinkslearning.com
www.keystoreadingsuccesss.com
or e-mail: info@keyslearning.com

Dedicated to
parents and teachers who devote their lives to helping their children and students be all they can be in life.

TABLE OF CONTENTS

FROM ADHD TO A'S: IMPROVE READING, MEMORY, AND LEARNING *QUICKLY* FOR KINESTHETIC LEARNERS
Ricki Linksman

Parents and teachers—does your child or teen have ADHD or ADD or is a kinesthetic learner? Are you frustrated because you do not know how to help him or her improve in reading, comprehension, learning, memory, studying, test-taking or raising grades? This eye-opening book packed with strategies to improve learning by author Ricki Linksman, accelerated brain-based learning and reading expert, can turn your frustration and hopelessness into relief and joy as you find that your child can learn and be successful!

For 39 years, Ricki Linksman has been helping tens of thousands of students worldwide with ADHD/ADD or who are kinesthetic learners achieve rapid success through the accelerated kinesthetic learning techniques she developed. Your search for solutions lies in this landmark book, *From ADHD to A's: Improve Reading Learning and Memory Quickly for Kinesthetic Learners*. Find out how you can help your child be a successful student, raise self-esteem and motivation, develop a life-long love of reading, and improve parent-child or teacher-child communication by knowing how your child learns and studies best! This work is two books in one: Part 1 is a book about Kinesthetic Right-brain Learners, and Part 2 is a book about Kinesthetic Left-brain Learners. Discover the key to your kinesthetic child's or teen's brain! A classic and timeless work every parent with a child of any age who is kinesthetic can cherish!

Final thought—if this book describes your child and you feel you would like further courses, books, material, coaching or help for a kinesthetic child visit me at:
National Reading Diagnostics Institute and Keys Learning
www.readinginstruction.com
www.keyslearning.com
www.keystolearningsuccess.com or
www.superlinkslearning.com

Introduction

FROM ADHD TO A'S

Has your child received a diagnosis of ADHD (Attention Deficit Hyperactivity Disorder) or ADD (Attention Deficit Disorder) or is being recommended for testing for that challenge? Are you wondering whether your child actually has an attention disorder or is simply a kinesthetic learner that needs to engage in gross motor (large-muscle) activity to learn best? Do you find that despite medication for ADHD or ADD your child is still not improving in reading, learning, grades, test scores, or study skills? Are you experiencing frustration at not knowing how to help your child improve? If so, you are not alone.

Among those struggling with learning, is a sub-group whose numbers are staggering—running into the millions. Of those, thousands and thousands of parents have personally shared with me for the past thirty-nine years their tremendous pain and frustration in not knowing how to help their child or teen diagnosed with ADHD or ADD, or suspected of having those challenges. Many express that their child seemed bright, inquisitive, and curious about learning, yet they received reports from school that they are struggling in school because they could have ADHD or ADD. Whether your child or teen is ultimately diagnosed by a medical doctor and put on medication for ADHD or ADD or not, the question remains: "Why is my child still struggling with reading, learning, comprehension, or memory?" If you find that your child either has ADHD or ADD or you or someone else suspects your child has that challenge, or your child has been labeled as such but you do not feel he or she really has that challenge, but you are still concerned about how to help your child or teen improve in school, then help is resting in your hands right now. I have written his book as a guide for you to help your child, starting immediately.

It is not hopeless. You **can** help your child improve in school, with reading, memory, learning and becoming an "A" student, whether your child has been diagnosed with ADHD or ADD, or you only feel he or she has that disorder, or you suspect your child has been misdiagnosed and does not really have ADHD or ADD.

Ask yourself this question: "Does your child only have trouble concentrating and focusing when doing school work, but has intense concentration when watching television, DVD's, and movies, playing video games, or engaging in sports?"

ADHD or ADD is not a selective disorder—either the child has it or not. If you feel your child only seems to be disengaged when it comes to school work or reading, but is quite focused when doing what he or she wants, have you ever considered that your child could be a kinesthetic learner? Whether or not he or she has ADHD or ADD, but likes to move a lot, your child can benefit from kinesthetic learning techniques. Once kinesthetic learners are given the opportunity to learn through the proper methods, their ADHD-like or ADD-like behaviors often disappear.

It is astounding how many students have been labeled "attention-deficit disordered." Years ago, only medical practitioners determined whether a child had an attention-deficit disorder, and the numbers were small. Now, teachers, relatives, and next-door neighbors are quick to point out the characteristics of ADHD or ADD in a child or teen. Increasing numbers of youngsters are routinely placed on "trials" of Ritalin or other medications without first ruling out other factors that could be causing apparent ADHD or ADD symptoms. A kinesthetic learner may not need medication so much as innovative teaching methods.

There are four basic types of learners: visual, auditory, tactile and kinesthetic. While types may overlap, visual learners tend to work best with visual stimuli, while auditory learners relate best to auditory techniques and verbal material. Tactile students absorb new information most readily through their sense of touch and their hands, such as through writing or drawing.

Kinesthetic learners, though, require body movement and action for optimal results. They need to move around and use their muscles to learn. They learn through action, doing, exploration, and discovery.

Kinesthetically oriented children find it stressful to be asked to "look and listen" for long periods. Imagine the frustration of having your hands tied, your mouth covered, and your eyes blindfolded so that you could not gesture, speak, or see. Kinesthetic students face similar frustration when not allowed to move in a classroom. To relieve stress, they seek to break out of these constraints. When faced with several hours of desk work, for which they are required to "sit still," they tend to get up to sharpen their pencil several times, they ask to go to the rest room, or they drop things, so they can get up to retrieve them. They may seek to be the class monitor or run errands just to have a break from sitting still. If they cannot engage in these activities, they will find other outlets for their muscles to move such as wiggling their legs, rocking or leaning back in their chairs, or throwing wads of paper into a waste paper basket. When reprimanded for these actions, they may resort to further misbehavior involving movement as part of a need to move. Teachers consider many of these behaviors as red flags for an attention (or behavioral) disorder, and they may not realize the child is merely a kinesthetic learner.

Another frustration that kinesthetic learners face is poor achievement. Any type of learner can be successful. However, of all the learning styles, kinesthetic learners are least likely to receive appropriate teaching methods. When reading is taught in the primary grades, most of the instruction involves the teacher talking (auditory) and using displays, either on the whiteboard or in books or handouts (visual). The teacher introduces new letters, words, or word families verbally and has the class repeat them (auditory), and write them (tactile). In kindergarten, students generally take part in group activities involving songs (auditory) with various actions (kinesthetic). Projects requiring large-muscle movement are also common at that level. However, from first grade on, seatwork predominates, and creative, kindergarten-type activities rapidly diminish. Even nowadays, with the pressure for students to do well on state or norm-referenced tests, some schools even have created an environment in kindergarten that looks more like the upper grades in which young students are also made to sit at their desks all day to focus on academics. Not coincidentally, it is at this point when kinesthetic techniques are eliminated in the classroom that teachers often start complaining about "ADHD or ADD behaviors" in some of their students.

Unfortunately, remedial reading instruction, tutoring, or even Special Ed or specific learning disabilities programs may not be successful if a student's learning type has not been properly identified. Frequently the approach is just "more of the same," using the same types of techniques as in the classroom. However, a thorough reading evaluation and a customized approach, matching the student's way of learning to instruction, however, often results in rapid progress.

At National Reading Diagnostics Institute and Keys Learning, for over twenty-three years, we have had dramatic success with kinesthetic learners using kinesthetic techniques. We use the Superlinks to Accelerated Learning™ Assessment (consisting of the Linksman Learning Style Assessment and Linksman Brain Hemispheric Preference Assessment) to determine a student's preferred and best way of learning. Then, we use Superlinks to Accelerated Learning™ and Keys to Reading Success™ brain-based accelerated learning techniques to teach through the child or teen's best and fastest learning style and brain style. Using these brain-based learning techniques, we improve memory, focus, and concentration and accelerate the speed of learning such subjects such as reading, comprehension, phonics, vocabulary, study skills, test-taking skills, and test prep for class and state reading tests and the ACT and SAT to apply to improved learning and grades in content area subjects.

As part of the diagnosis, not only do we identify one's learning style, but we also identify one's brain hemispheric preference. For over thirty-nine years, I have identified large differences in the way someone who has a kinesthetic left-brain preference thinks, learns, and remembers compared to someone who has a kinesthetic right-brain preference. This is true of the other learning styles. Thus, I have coined the term "Superlinks" to differentiate between visual left-brain learners and visual right-brain learners, auditory left-brain and auditory right-brain learners, tactile left-brain and tactile right-brain learners, and kinesthetic left-brain and kinesthetic right-brain learners. It is important to know whether someone is a kinesthetic right-brain learner or a kinesthetic left-brain learner to accelerate learning, improve reading and comprehension, and boost one's memory.

It is important to realize that students of any learning style and brain style—not only kinesthetic learners-- can have ADHD or ADD. It is also critical to know that any student having any learning style preference can be made to look like they have symptoms of ADHD or ADD when he or she is not taught in his or her best or fastest way of learning. For example, if you take visual learners and teach them without showing them visual materials, they will start to act distracted or lose focus during a purely auditory lesson. Similarly, those who are auditory learners who need auditory lessons but are denied the ability to listen and talk and are made to do only "silent" work can also show symptoms of distractibility and lack of focus. Someone who is tactile and needs to write and use his or hands can demonstrate symptoms of ADHD or ADD when made to sit still with hands folded during a lesson. It does not mean they have ADHD or ADD but their symptoms may mimic ADHD or ADD because they are not being taught in their best, fastest, and most effective way of learning. That is the reason that it is critical to know each child's or teen's best way of learning, or Superlink to Accelerated Learning. ™ By knowing the child's Superlink, parents and teachers can intervene by making sure their symptoms of distractibility, hyperactivity, lack of focus or concentration, or academic struggles are really due to ADHD/ADD or are due merely to a mismatch between their best and fastest way of learning and how instruction is being delivered to them in class or at home. If you are not sure the student has ADHD or ADD or is merely a kinesthetic learner, you can try interventions. See if the student's learning improves by altering the method of teaching. This will help rule out if the child or teen is showing ADHD or ADD symptoms merely because of a mismatch between instructional methods and how the child needs to learn through his or her Superlink learning preference. To identify someone's Superlink, one can go to http://www.superlinkslearning.com or get more information about it at http://www.readinginstruction.com and take the test I developed online. The student may have taken a learning style test already and you think you know the student's preference, but the Superlinks test also identifies the *combination* of learning style and brain style preference, which is critical because the way we process and store information in the brain also impacts learning. As you will learn from this book, there is a difference between kinesthetic right-brain learners and kinesthetic left-brain learners. Similarly, there are also vast differences between visual left-brain learners and visual right-brain learners, auditory left-brain learners and auditory right-brain learners, and tactile left-brain learners and tactile right-brain learner, which are covered in my other books.

It has always pained me deeply to see the frustration of parents and their children when they struggle with learning. As an educator, it would break my heart to see children who should be excited about life and learning carry the heavy burden of failure on their little shoulders. When you hear the student express that he or she feels dumb or stupid because they cannot seem to learn or read like everyone else, it is heart-breaking.

One of the saddest memory etched in my brain was of a little boy I observed as I visited different classrooms in my role as a reading specialist. When I first saw him at the start of the school year he had bright, eager eyes and a big smile as he bounced into school, excited to be there to learn. Then, to see him a few moments later struggling with reading as he sees the other children doing well was painful to watch. Day by day, his smile disappeared and his shoulders became hunched over and he walked with his head looking down at the ground. The heaviness thickened day after day, and in talking to him, he said, "I'm stupid. There must be something wrong with me." How could this enthusiastic child, thrilled to be in school, suddenly feel like a failure within a few months? The little excited child who entered kindergarten or first grade but discovered he could not succeed like the others began to feel the pain of failure. This scenario is all too often played out in many schools and homes. With time, there are meetings between parents and teachers, interventions tried, but the child is still not keeping up with the other children. Soon, the child starts the journey from either special testing in school to see if he or she has a learning disability, or he or she is sent to a doctor or specialist outside of school to see if he or she has ADHD or ADD. The child's self-esteem drops as he or she feels there is something wrong with him or her. Some of them silently accept that they have something wrong, while others try to hide their failure by getting attention from negative means such as acting out, being the class clown, or dropping out. A cycle of failure is set in place, and if this is not reversed, many children become behavior problems, withdraw, give up, and even drop out as soon as they are old enough to do so. I have seen this tragedy enacted time and again in a lifetime of working in schools and with parents outside of school. The good news is that this situation can be prevented, and if it does happen, it is reversible! How do I know? I have personally intervened in cases of students of all ages both in schools and outside of school and turned their failures into successes. In fact, the success has been so dramatic, that I have been able to turn around entire failing schools within less than a school year.

The pain of seeing a child when he or she is left back a year, pulled out, or put in special classes left such a deep impression on me that I devoted my entire career to finding a way to end their pain. I made an in-depth study of the latest brain research to find out how to apply it to helping students learn. I was one of the first people in the country, back in the 1970's, to apply brain research to learning to learn and learning to read. When I put it to the test with failing students, I marveled at the phenomenal results. I was taking entire classes of failing students destined to be left back and bringing them to success in reading where they met requirements within as little time as two months. Many of them were failing because they had special needs, had ADHD or ADD, or were just not learning at the speed everyone else in their class was learning. Soon, I was taking entire schools from failure to success within the course of a school year. As word spread of this success, parents began flocking to me to help their child as well. When I read a report in 1993 published by the U.S. Department of Education that said that two-thirds of the nation's students in grade 4, 8 and 12 could not read at grade level, I was horrified. I knew from the parents and teachers in my area that this was happening, but this was shocking to hear that this was a national epidemic. It was not the numbers that were as devastating as thinking that each of those statistics represented another child or teen's face with that pain of failure written all over it, and the utter frustration of their parents in not knowing how to help their child. These numbers represented another child who would turn out like the many I had seen who would act out, tune out, or drop out. To me, it translated into the numerous cases of child and teen crime destroying our nation. Having worked with many teens whose journey into crime began with school failure and as a way to find acceptance from someone in their life, even if were a gang, I saw each statistic of failure as another potential child who would be lost. The good news is that I have consistently reversed the lives of children or teens heading down the road of criminal or gang activity by helping them be successful. They were able to see that they were not failures, but as smart and bright as everyone else. When they realized that they could achieve, there was a total transformation, and they became not only good students, but top students. They had not turned to gangs and crime because they were "bad" kids; they were hungry for love and acceptance, and if they could not get it from their academic life, they would find it elsewhere. By helping them achieve in school, their need for acceptance and success reversed the cycle of failure and put them back on track to success.

Wanting to help all those children and teens from leading a life of failure to achieving success and ending their parents' frustration, I founded a parent-child and teacher training institute, National Reading Diagnostics Institute, shortly after reading about that Dept. of Education's study so that parents could learn how they can reverse their child or teen's failure. As word spread nationally, schools around the country also brought me in to help train their teachers in the techniques I developed to bring students from failure to success in the shortest possible time.

It has been the passion and joy of my life to see a child and a teen who is burdened with the weight of failure be freed of that pain and convert it to the joy of success. To help parents and children still suffering this pain of not knowing how to get help and who are in need of solutions, especially rapid ones, I have made available these techniques through training parents and teachers, and sharing these methods in books, resources, online resources, software programs, ebooks, online webinars, and teleseminars.

I have filled the book with strategies, activities, and example lessons to help you get started in adapting instruction to the learner's kinesthetic Superlink learning style. For each chapter, strategies, tips, example lessons, and ideas are given for you to try with the child or teen. There are hundreds of tips, examples, strategies and activities to try in this book. These are just a small sampling of over ten thousand pages of activities I have developed over thirty-nine years for not only kinesthetic left-brain and kinesthetic right-brain learners, but also for visual left-brain and visual right-brain learners, auditory left-brain and auditory right-brain learners, and tactile left-brain and tactile right-brain learners. Some of these activities are from my many pre-K, K-12, and college courses in reading, comprehension, phonics, fluency, vocabulary, study skills, memory skills, test-taking, and test prep courses, including state reading tests and for the ACT and SAT. These activities can be adapted for students in regular education, gifted, special education, Title 1, remedial reading, ESL, or bilingual programs, and for students with ADHD, ADD, or dyslexia.

Since every child or teen takes different courses from each other, the book provides activities, examples, and strategies that can be applied to *whatever school work or homework the child or teen is doing*. It can also be applied to reading for enjoyment or to reading material related to the child or teen's hobbies.

Knowing one's Superlink preference and learning through those Superlinks methods can accelerate learning. After years of working with tens of thousands of students, it is clear that when teaching through techniques that do not match one's style, it makes learning slower and more difficult. Switch to the right method and the difference in learning speed and effectiveness is dramatic!

These Superlinks techniques have proven to help children from pre-K, K-12, college, whether in regular education, special education, gifted, bi-lingual or ESOL or ESL, reading remedial, Title 1, or those who have ADHD or ADD. Adults have also benefitted from these techniques to improve in learning whether for a job, new career, or professional development in any field. Athletes and coaches have used these techniques even to improve in sports.

An ounce of prevention, in the form of instruction matched to learning preferences, is worth years of remediation or special programs using inappropriate techniques.

If the student of any age, whether pre-K, K-12, college, or adult, is predominately a kinesthetic right-brain learner or a kinesthetic left-brain learner this book provides you with understanding about his or her characteristics as a learner, best methods to use to accelerate learning, how to communicate with him or her, and how he or she learns, thinks, reads, and remembers. It is jam-packed with activities to try to improve reading, memory, and learning quickly for kinesthetic learners.

Once you know the basic accelerated learning kinesthetic strategies, you can apply them to help the student learn anything better and faster. The line of resources I developed, such as books, e-books, live and online courses, software, and distance learning and coaching, has helped tens of thousands of parents and teachers help their children, including students in entire schools and districts, accelerate learning for all types of learners. It is my hope that it also helps the student learn and improve.

Here are some further resources containing strategies for students with ADHD or ADD, or who are kinesthetic learners, either right-brain or left-brain preferences, or those who are of all learning style preferences but are not being taught in their best way of learning, causing them to be frustrated or to struggle:

Reading Resources for Kinesthetic Learners:

Kinesthetic Reading Comprehension
(Kinesthetic Virtual Reality Reading)
(includes Literal and Inferential Comprehension)

Kinesthetic Vocabulary

Kinesthetic Phonics (Off the Wall Phonics)

Kinesthetic Test-taking Prep
(includes kinesthetic test prep for class tests, state
reading tests, high school placement tests; or the ACT or SAT)

Kinesthetic Memory and Study Skills

If you are not sure if the student is a kinesthetic right-brain learner or a kinesthetic left-brain learner, or any other learning style and brain style or combination of several, and you want to be sure, you can give the student an assessment to find out. To make it easy for you, I created an online test to help you discover the student's fastest way of learning at: **http://www.superlinkslearning.com**. The student can take the Superlinks test online to find his or her specific way of learning. Matching the learner to the right techniques accelerates success.

As a special bonus, readers can enter a special discount listed at the end of this book.

One final thought—if this book describes the learner and you feel you would like further courses, books, digital books, audio, material, trainings, coaching or help for a kinesthetic learner, contact me at any of the following websites:

http://www.keyslearning.com
http://www.readinginstruction.com
http://www.keystoreadingsuccess.com

These techniques, strategies, activities, and sample lessons have proven to help tens of thousands of parents and teachers end their frustration in not knowing how to help their kinesthetic child or student, either with or without ADHD or ADD. It is my hope that you too will find instant relief and put the kinesthetic right-brain learner or kinesthetic left-brain learner on the road to success.

-Ricki Linksman
March 2016

CHAPTER 1: DIFFERENCES IN HOW PEOPLE WITH DIFFERENT LEARNING STYLES PERCEIVE THE WORLD

Why do we have a preference for one mode of learning over another? It is all about the technology of the brain. What form of stimulation did we receive more of as we were growing up? Did our caretakers give us many objects, pictures, mobiles, or illustrated books at which to look? Was there much talking, conversation, dialogue, or music in our childhood? Maybe we were given a great amount of hands-on activities to do like finger-painting, stringing beads, coloring, or toys that required the use of our hands and fingers. Were we encouraged to be more actively engaged in running, jumping, crawling, swimming, playing ball, building with blocks, making play-houses, or doing competitive activities? Whatever stimulation we received, our brains were grooving pathways along those lines. Over time, those networks of sensory pathways became more firmly established and more automatic. When something is automatic we do not have to think about it—it comes easily. Thus, we feel more comfortable and learn how to learn faster when working through that modality.

Over thirty years of interviewing and assessing the learning style and brain style preferences of people from all walks of life, there are certain patterns of behavior, thought, comprehension, and memory that identify those who have one sensory preference over another. Let us take the scenario of a person entering a room. The experience is different for people who have a different learning style preference. The information that comes in, how the person comprehends the experience, and how he or she remembers it is different for people of various learning styles. Of course, there are people who learn through a combination of two or more learning styles and some who use all of them! Depending upon the preference, or the combination, that room provides a different experience for each of them.

The World According to a Kinesthetic Learner

If a child has had much stimulation through movement of his or her body and large muscles, then that pathway becomes more comfortable for that learner. When this person enters a room, the first question that arises is, "What can I do here?" This person looks for space to move around, physical activities that can be done, and some challenge by which a goal can be achieved or won. When processing the experience, this person focuses on the action in the room. When trying to remember the room, this person best remembers what he or she did in the room. They then develop a preference for being a kinesthetic learner.

Learning Style Alone is Only Part of the Process

Besides taking in information through our fastest learning style, the information is further processed in the brain. Some people process things in a sequential or step-by-step order. Others process information by getting the big picture or main idea first and then fitting in the details. Medical researchers have previously identified sequential thinking processes take place in the left side of the brain, and the global overview thinking processes happen in the right side of the brain. Whether one subscribes to that distinction or not, or as brain research identifies exactly where they take place, for the purposes of defining the two types of processing, sequential thinking is referred to in this book as "left-brain," while global thinking is referred to as "right-brain." Whether science later proves sequential thought is somewhere else does not matter so much as knowing that we want to learn new things sequentially as opposed to learning new things through a global overview that does not focus on steps in order. The technique of teaching that matches how we learn is what matters most when we are learning, no matter what terms are used for them, or where they are actually taking place in the brain.

Similarly, besides the order in which we process information, we also process through words or images. Some people think more in words. They talk to themselves and think about what is happening through language. Some people think more in terms of pictures. They perceive images, colors, shapes, designs, faces, and patterns and remember these the best. Some process equally through both. Again, whether words vs. graphics or pictures are actually localized in one part of the brain is not as important as knowing that is how we process information faster. For the sake and ease of terminology, in this book, in recognition that brain science is identifying multiple areas of the brain in which various processes take place, processing through words will be referred to as "left-brain" functioning; and processing through images or pictures will be referred to as "right-brain" functioning. Knowing whether we need text or pictures when we learn can help us accelerate our comprehension, memory, and mastery of a subject, irrespective of the parts of the brain in each individual case such functions are actually taking place.

The Superlink is the Combination of the Learning Style and Brain Hemispheric Preference

In the early 1970s, work was done regarding learning styles. In those days, people were classified as one of three styles: visual, auditory, and kinesthetic. Later, the term tactile was lumped in with kinesthetic, keeping the classification as three styles. In over thirty years of work, I was one of the few who recognized that a tactile learner is extremely different from a kinesthetic learner. Tactile and kinesthetic learners are two distinct types of learners and have different learning needs. Thus, I separate learning styles into four categories. In the early 1980s, as I used learning style teaching methods and techniques to teach people, I also observed repeatedly that visual learners were not all the same. I realize that some visual learners focused on printed words in text, while others focused on pictures, images, and graphics.

This same phenomena occurred with auditory learners. Some auditory learners were great at memorizing lectures, while other auditory learners could not repeat a word of a lecture in a university hall if their life depended on it. Yet, they may have been highly aware of sounds, music, and sound effects.

I also realized that not all tactile learners were alike. Some focused on writing words, while others were not good at writing but excelled in drawing or making hands-on projects. Some were able to express their feelings in words, while others expressed their feelings through nonverbal communication.

Finally, not all kinesthetic people were alike. Some liked to learn by verbal instructions, and others got annoyed when anyone spoke when they were engaged in activity. They preferred instead nonverbal demonstration that they could copy. Some kinesthetic people liked to talk about what they did, while others did not want to talk at all about the physical experiences in which they engaged.

Through these observations, I discovered that some visual learners were left-brain thinkers, while other visual learners were right-brain thinkers. There were visual left-brain learner who learned faster by seeing text; and there were visual right-brain learners who learned faster by seeing pictures or graphics. The same was true of the other learning styles. I saw dramatic increases in learning speed when the learning style and brain hemispheric preference techniques were combined. I thus coined the term "superlink" to describe the combination of one's learning style and brain hemispheric preference. I thus named the strategies as the Superlinks to Accelerated Learning™. Since the 1980s, I have tracked the use of Superlinks in the teaching of reading with entire bodies of students in schools, from elementary school, to middle school and high school, and to college students, and adults in various professions. Without fail, people were able to learn faster and master any subject when taught in their superlink style—the combination of learning style and brain hemispheric preference style.

This accelerated system of learning was so effective, I created an entire pre-K, kindergarten, grade one through grade twelve, and college and adult reading curriculum program based on this Superlinks to Accelerated Learning™ and named it Keys to Reading Success™. This method has been studied and researched and have proven time and again to raise reading levels of 88%-99% of all students in a school anywhere from two, three, four, or five grade reading levels—on average—within months. The longest time for these gains to take place has been six to eight months, and has occurred as rapidly as two to four months' time. This includes students who are in regular education, gifted, special education, Title I, or remedial reading programs, students with ADHD and ADD, and students who need to learn English who are in ELL (English language learners), ESL or ESOL (English as a Second Language), or bilingual or dual language programs. It works to improve reading levels in both males and female. It works for people of all cultures or language groups. It works for people of all ages, from the very young to adults who have retired. Using the Superlinks to Accelerated Learning™ technique with the Keys to Reading Success™ reading comprehension and memory improvement program has helped students become top readers, to comprehend what they read, to remember what was read for an assignment or test, and to retain in long-term memory what was read for mastery in any field.

For this reason, it is recommended that one take both the Superlinks Learning Style Preference Assessment™ tests and the Brain Hemispheric Preference Assessment™ inventory tests for the most complete and comprehension diagnosis of one's best and fastest way of learning.

Knowing the Learning Style Can Speed Up Learning

As our brain takes in the world through the filter of our learning style, or combination of styles, that network of thinking is easier to use for comprehending, learning, and remembering. In our unique learning style, we take in information faster, focus on comprehending and thinking about what we learned, and recall and memorize the material better. These variations in strategies can help us learn how to learn any subject faster. If we know our own unique way of learning, we can use that information to help us learn how to learn any subject more rapidly. It will open doors for us to learn more and learn more rapidly. Knowing the keys to our own brain can help us ask for what we need from an instructor, and if not provided by that teacher, help us provide for ourselves the strategy to master any subject. If the learning environment in which we find ourselves does not match the way we learn faster, we will have some strategies to use by ourselves to "translate" any subject into the way we need to learn it so we are independent and can learn, even on our own.

I developed the Virtual Reality Reading™ comprehension and memory improvement strategies to help the learner take in information that is read in their best and fastest way of learning. Once they know this technique, it forms the basis of many other comprehension tasks, study skills, memory skills, and test taking skills. The learner can use this virtual reality reading comprehension technique to effective learn anything quickly.

Beyond this technique, there are many other skills and teaching methods needed to master any subject. Building on the virtual reality comprehension and memory techniques is a series of reading comprehension practice skills, study skills, note taking skills, and test taking skills. These are all designed to increase comprehension and memory of whatever one is learning.

CHAPTER 2: WHAT IS A KINESTHETIC LEFT-BRAIN LEARNER AND HOW TO IMPROVE MEMORY, READING COMPREHENSION, NOTE TAKING, STUDY, AND TEST TAKING SKILLS TO LEARN ANYTHING QUICKLY?

What Is a Kinesthetic Left-Brain Learner?

Kinesthetic left-brain learners learn quickly and can improve reading comprehension and memory through movement and action of their body and large motor muscles in an organized, systematic way. Because the language function is in the left side of the brain, they can verbalize movement activities in systematic, structured ways.

Kinesthetic left-brain learners need to move a great deal and are restless when they have to stay in one place. If they are forced to stay in one seat too long, they will begin to move or rock in the seat, kick their legs, or get out of the seat spontaneously. Others may be distracted by their movements. Yet if they are given an opportunity to use their body, they will actually stick to a task with great concentration; it is when they are denied movement that they find some other outlet for their kinesthetic needs that may not be productive. They are going to move anyway, whether they are restricted or not—so at least their lessons should be structured in a way that includes movement as a positive part of their training.

They like team sports, organized games, or exercises that have rules and are done in a step-by-step way. Many kinesthetic left-brain people are extremely coordinated and can time their movements to be in synch with others. They may excel in synchronous swimming, gymnastics, acrobatics, or choreographed dance.

Not all kinesthetic left-brain people are athletic and coordinated, but they still require sequential movement activities in other fields, whether they are developing real estate, designing a software program or app, find a cure for a disease, or exploring a new hobby. Movement for them can be just mentally moving from one topic or project to another. They are systematic and orderly and tend to stick to and complete a task before moving on.

They need room to move around and comfortable sitting areas to stretch out and relax. If a place does not allow them to move about or has no action-oriented activity, kinesthetic left-brain people will feel uncomfortable and bored because there is nothing for them to do there.

They enjoy talking with other people while in motion or physically doing something, such as jogging, exercising, or working with someone else.

How Kinesthetic Left-Brain Learners Can Improve Memory, Reading Comprehension, Note Taking, Study, and Test-Taking Skills to Learn Anything Quickly

Kinesthetic left-brain learners can improve their memory, reading comprehension, study skills, note taking and test taking skills to learn quickly by using an organized, systematic, step-by-step approach that involves moving their bodies and muscles. They are language-oriented, so they can describe what they are doing and follow verbal systematic directions for movement activities. They can get on an exercise bike and read or study while pedaling, or walk around the room while memorizing the lines to a play. Learning games, simulations, role-playing and competitions are great ways for them to learn. Whatever movement they do, they prefer to use a formula, structure, or outline for their work.

It may appear to others that kinesthetic left-brain people are not listening because they are constantly moving, and they process thought better when their eyes are down and away from a speaker, but they are attentive when they are in motion. It is so stressful for them to sit still with their eyes on a speaker that they cannot concentrate on listening. Yet when they are moving about, they are relaxed, comfortable, and attentive.

Hands-on materials and manipulatives are important to kinesthetic learners, but they benefit more from moving their entire bodies, not just their hands. The simple act of standing up helps them learn because it gets their legs, arms, and other muscles moving. They need to write with large markers or chalk on a flip chart, white board, or chalkboard while standing. Doing math problems or outlining a report on a flip chart helps them to think better. By writing in large letters on a whiteboard, they can involve their arm muscles and the activity into the kinesthetic realm. Kinesthetic left-brain people do not prefer to doodle or draw as tactile learners do, but they may do so only when it is the only movement they are permitted in a constrained work or learning situation. It offers them some movement of their arm and hands, which may not fully satisfy them but it is better than sitting still.

In whatever subject they learn, kinesthetic left-brain learners need to learn by doing something in a sequential way. Just listening to lectures and verbal explanations is not enough for them to assimilate the material. They can benefit by volunteering to be a how-to demonstrator instead of just watching a demonstration. If they hear action words in sequential order, they will physically understand the material. They need a coach who will actively work through the steps of a process. If they are learning how to use a computer, they have to be at a computer while going through each step. If they are learning about carpentry, they will need the tools and materials so as the instructor models for them how to build something they can do it as they learn. They will remember not what an instructor does, but what *they* do.

When doing study skills or note taking to memorize material for a test or examination, they recall what they did with the material. For study skills, kinesthetic left-brain learners need to act out or dramatize the material, either physically or in their mind, so they can remember what their body did or what they imagined doing. If the subject is math or science, they need to work out the problems or experiments in a step-by-step way in real-life applications, for example, by doing the math required for sending a spaceship to the moon, mixing chemicals to produce medicine, or writing a software program. If circumstances do not allow a kinesthetic left-brain learner to do an activity, their next best resort is to watch activity—movies on television or in a theater, using streaming video, or watching a program on the Internet or on any electronic device, preferably sequentially-presented programs.

Another kinesthetic method for them is to visualize themselves in their mind moving. In this way they can experience the action within themselves without being noticeable to others. They should feel in their mind that their body is moving or enacting whatever it is they are trying to learn, even while their physical body remains still. This will also activate neuronal growth in their brain as if they had actually physically performed the action.

Kinesthetic left-brain learners thrive on achievement, winning, challenges, and discovery. Being goal-oriented, they enjoy the thrill of the game, and their motivation increases in a competitive environment. They like competing with themselves and beating their own record or against teams. Since the left side of the brain handles facts and figures, kinesthetic left-brainers tend to discuss game scores or keep records of achievement of others or themselves. Converting any learning experience into a competitive game helps kinesthetic left-brain people learn better.

Kinesthetic left-brain learners need manipulatives; organized games; building materials; sports equipment, such as balls, basketball hoops, jump ropes, and exercise bikes; science projects; large markers to write on large pieces of paper, flip charts, or white boards; computers; musical instruments; hands-on models; kits; or real objects to move. They like high action yet structured programs, games, and apps on the computer or any electronic digital device.

Kinesthetic left-brain learners can read, work, or study with or without music. Moving or dancing to the rhythm and beat of music can stimulate them to work better. When their muscles are in motion, stress is reduced, their attention and motivation increase, and they learn faster. Kinesthetic left-brain people enjoy playing musical instruments that engage the whole body. They can handle a systematic approach to learning an instrument and will attend to the technical aspects of playing, such as timing, rhythm, and reading music.

Working in cooperative groups or teams helps the kinesthetic left-brain learner because they can move around from group to group. They like to work from a plan or structured outline, so they know each step of the process beforehand. Interaction with different people in different groups fulfills their need to be where the action is.

To improve memory, reading comprehension, study skills, note taking, and test taking skills to learn anything quickly, kinesthetic left-brain learners should get actively involved in the reading material, either by physically acting out the text or imaging themselves doing so. They should imagine experiencing their muscles moving by acting out in their mind what the words describe in sequential order. To engage their interest and remember what they read, kinesthetic left-brain learners need to convert the words into an action movie in their mind in which they are part of the action. They tend to forget whatever they do not imagine themselves "doing" in their mind as they read.

Kinesthetic left-brain learners prefer to read action-packed books. They like to read about movement-oriented activities in a detailed, step-by-step, well-organized way if it can help them improve what they do. The left-brain's ability to think in terms of language helps them understand verbal or written directions for action-oriented subjects. They enjoy "how-to" books that help them perform better if written in logical, sequential ways. Business people enjoy reading how-to suggestions for improving their businesses. Sports lovers enjoy books that help them perfect their techniques.

Kinesthetic left-brain learners need a purpose and action-oriented reason to be motivated to read. If they know their sales will increase if they read the training manual, they will be sure to read it. If they know they need to pass the driver's license examination, they will force themselves to read the manual.

In the work place, kinesthetic left-brain people can be found in jobs that require movement along with left-brain organization, putting what they do into words, or giving detailed verbal directions to others. Jobs that require traveling, speaking, and being clear and organized in one's presentation are found in sales, marketing, district management, owning a self-employed business, teaching, and training. Kinesthetic left-brain people who go into the sciences may be involved in experiments, research and laboratory work, or medical fields, becoming doctors and nurses.

Since they excel at movement jobs that are related to being on time, a function of the left side of the brain, they may be pilots, train conductors, chauffeurs, truck drivers, delivery people, or parcel, express mail, or postal workers. Work that involves the physical body and using details, measurements, and precision are construction, engineering, roadwork, farming, painting, wallpapering, plumbing, electrical work, cleaning, furniture crafting, and doing repair work. Jobs that require physically protecting other people and that use the left-brain attention to structure, organization, and rules are in areas such as the armed forces, such as in the Army, the Navy, the Coast Guard or the Marines, or in the police force, fire department, or secret service.

Kinesthetic left-brain learners may be involved in organized sports and games or may use their verbal abilities to become sportscasters or coaches and instructors in movement fields such as aerobics, exercise, or dance. They may write action stories, sports columns, reviews of movies, dance, or theatrical performances, or organized and structured how-to books. Their ability to visualize action on a screen or stage may make them good screenwriters and playwrights. As artists, they are structured and systematic in their work and will portray detailed action through illustrations, cartoons, comic strips, or commercials for advertising. They may be directors of movies, plays, or dance groups. They may become actors and actresses, musicians, performers, or instructors of performing arts that require body movement.

Adapting Learning to a Kinesthetic Left-Brain Style

Kinesthetic left-brain learners should ask instructors to let them do movement activities in a sequential way to learn the material. If instruction is presented as a lecture, they need to ask for outlines or study guides or do their own note taking in sequential order, so they can convert the words into: a) actions; b) a movie in their mind in which they imagine themselves doing the action; or c) an outline while they stand up and write it in large size on a flip chart or white board. They can find sequential material, either written and in audio-visual format that relates to the subject and convert the text into a physical action or an imagined action in their mind.

CHAPTER 3: WHAT IS A KINESTHETIC RIGHT-BRAIN LEARNER AND HOW TO IMPROVE MEMORY, READING COMPREHENSION, NOTE TAKING, STUDY, AND TEST TAKING SKILLS TO LEARN ANYTHING QUICKLY?

What Is A Kinesthetic Right-Brain Learner?

Kinesthetic right-brain learners can improve memory, reading comprehension, note taking, study and test taking skills to learn quickly through moving their gross motor muscles in a creative, imaginative, free-flowing, and unstructured way. They do not think in words, but get information intuitively.

They become highly restless if forced to stay still or remain in one place too long. Kinesthetic left-brain learners will feel so constrained and physically stressed that they will start to move around anyway. Their need to keep moving and changing activities may make they look hyperactive to others. It is actually when they are denied movement that they look distracted. It is better to give them movement activities related to the learning task, such as learning games, exercises, or simulations. They will then be able to concentrate as well as people of other styles do when working in their element. Unless given productive activities related to their work, they will kick or swing their legs under the table, drum on the tabletop, slouch, rock in their seats, or find excuses to get up, whether it is to get a snack or look out a window.

Not all kinesthetic right-brain learners are athletes. There are many other activities that involve movement. For them, movement can be moving in their mind from one topic or project to another.

Kinesthetic right-brain learners can think about several things simultaneously and can have many projects going on at once. They can keep each one straight in their minds without any difficulty. They work in an impulsive, quick way, wanting to see results immediately so they can move on to another activity. In the rush to complete a project, they may not worry about whether the parts were done to perfection. They see the whole picture, not the details.

There are times when they consider a job done just by having thought of it. Some kinesthetic right-brain people put the idea out, do some preliminary work, and move on to another project. It is up to the detail-oriented people around them to pick up the pieces and complete the task so they can then move on to create new inventions. They have a wealth of new ideas and discoveries, like a brainstorm session in motion, giving the world a seeming endless supply of novel, unique ideas.

Being goal-oriented, kinesthetic right-brain learners have the ability to get things done, handling many projects at once. They are not time-oriented, so they do not tend to stick to schedules, routines, or time constraints. They are go-with-the-flow people who will do what they feel like at the moment. They can keep work moving and be a wealth of creativity and imagination, although others have to be willing to accept their lack of consciousness of time. At work, as frequently as they arrive late, they may also become so absorbed in a task that they may stay overtime just to complete it, giving them more productivity than what they are paid to do!

A kinesthetic right-brain learner needs a comfortable environment, full of activity, with room to stretch out and move. Some will get up and leave if they are bored or in a restricted environment. Being outdoors is high on their list because there they can move freely.

Kinesthetic right-brain people enjoy being with other people when they can do something together that does not require a lot of talk. Watch them during a football game and you may hear grunts, moans, or cheers. They can communicate action without speaking and use their body and arms to dramatize or express what they want to describe. When they do talk, they use short action words and get to the point quickly.

How Kinesthetic Right-Brain Learners Can Improve Memory, Reading Comprehension, Note Taking, Study and Test Taking Skills to Learn Anything Quickly

Kinesthetic right-brain people can their improve memory, reading comprehension, note taking, study and test taking skills to learn quickly by moving in an unstructured, imaginative, and free-flowing way. They need to use their bodies and muscles to learn. Thus, they can learn better while cycling on a stationary bike, memorizing material by jumping rope, simulating or role-playing a situation, performing experiments, or playing creative games.

Kinesthetic right-brain learners, often adventuresome and daring, enjoy challenges. This group just needs to jump in and "do it." They pick up the how-to information by intuition or gut feelings and learn by trial and error, exploration, and discovery. They fully grasp the overall patterns of any situation and know what to do. Their excellent visual-spatial relations, intuition, and quick reflexes enable them to look at a problem, instantaneously judge a situation, and move accordingly, without words or written directions, to find the solution.

Kinesthetic right-brain learners do not require step-by-step, detailed instructions. They are whole-to-part learners who need to see the big picture or overview first and fill in the details later. For example, they will not give a detailed verbal account of a sports event—they will give the highlights and the winning score: the bottom line. If they see an entire math problem worked out with the answer and several examples, they can figure out how to solve similar problems.

Kinesthetic right-brain learners listen better to others while in motion, with their eyes focused down and away from the speaker. They remember more when they are in motion than when they are sitting still. When they are moving, they can relax, concentrate, and absorb information better.

They learn better by standing up to work. Writing on a flip chart or whiteboard with large markers works better for them than writing while sitting. By involving their whole arm, legs, and body, they can put the activity into the kinesthetic realm. Making a mind map of material they need to know by using their whole arm to write provides more activity and helps them recall what they learned. They doodle not because of a tactile need to write but because it offers more movement than sitting still.

They need active real life or simulated experiences. For example, when learning about accounting they would prepare a budget for a real company or an imaginary one they created for this learning experience. If volunteers are needed for a demonstration, kinesthetic right-brain learners jump at a chance to get out of their seats and do something. If they are learning a dance, they will remember it not by watching someone else do it, but by doing it themselves. They need to immerse themselves fully in the experience in an unstructured way. Many of them do not want long explanations; they want to figure something out for themselves. They need teachers who will take on the role of a coach, use only key action words, and guide them if they ask for help.

If a situation does not permit the kinesthetic right-brain learner to do an activity, their next resort is to watch activity on television, DVDs, videos, or movies. To remember what they learn, they need to act out the material or visualize themselves dramatizing it as if a movie were playing in their head. When they visualize they need to feel the movement in their muscles. Their body may move and sway as they go through the movements in their mind. When they receive directions to drive to a friend's house, they experience themselves turning the car right or left, or whipping along the curve in the road in their mind.

Good learning materials for a kinesthetic right-brain learner are manipulatives, games, building materials, tools, sports equipment, balls, exercise bikes, large flip charts whiteboards, large markers, computers with action games, percussion instruments, guitars or organs, rhythmic music, hands-on models, or real objects to move. They like unstructured, nonsequential, high-action, fast-moving video games, apps, and interactive programs. If a computer program is too slow or too structured, they become bored. They prefer moving a mouse, joystick, or swiping their fingers across a screen rather than using keystrokes on a keyboard.

Competitions and challenges interest kinesthetic right-brain people, either in games or on the job. They may participate in contests that determine who can sell or produce the most. They are goal-oriented and enjoy the thrill of winning points for themselves or their team. Make a game of anything and they will learn it.

Kinesthetic right-brain learners do better using note taking, study skills and test taking strategies by remembering what action they *did* while learning. For them to concentrate, distractions caused by the movement of others have to be eliminated. Working in a study carrel, using a divider, or facing a wall can keep them from noticing the movement of others, but they have to be comfortable while studying. Being stretched out on the floor or couch gives their muscles freedom of movement. They can work and study with or without music. Because they do not listen to the words, music does not interfere with their reading. The rhythm or beat stimulates their muscles to move or dance in time to the music. Their stress is reduced and their attention and motivation increases.

By working in cooperative groups, kinesthetic right-brain learners have an opportunity to move around more from group to group. They thrive on change and on interacting with different people to satisfy their need for action.

To improve memory and reading comprehension, kinesthetic right-brain learners need to convert words into a movie in which they are part of the action. Imagining that they are the director of a movie and converting the book or script into action scenes, while describing the action that would appear on their movie screen, will make a book come alive for them. Whatever they do not feel themselves doing—or imagining they are doing—as they read will be lost to their memory.

They read for the main idea or big picture, skipping small details, and are impatient with too many words. Thus, they tend to miss reading comprehension questions that deal with details, time sequence, or abstract ideas. It is not that they cannot remember the details, but they need kinesthetic right-brain techniques to master them.

Kinesthetic right-brain learners prefer short or highly action-packed books or how-to books that help them perform better. Unlike their left-brain counterparts, they need diagrams, photographs, or illustrations. They do not like to read a book from cover to cover but tend to skip around, getting what they need from it. They may learn by just looking at the pictures, glancing at the captions, or flipping through the pages, catching stray sentences that may give them all they need to know about a topic. They have an intuitive sense that helps them find what they need.

Kinesthetic right-brain learners need to know the end product before they start. Thus, they need to know the reason they are reading something. They will be motivated if they feel it will help them do something better. Watch them zip through a book if they feel it will help them be the top in their field, boost their sales, or get a promotion. Books with summaries or key points at the beginning or end of the chapter help them find what is important and relevant to them.

In the workforce, kinesthetic right-brain people can be found in jobs that require movement and frequent change. They may not attend to details, but they will work quickly to get a job done rapidly. With this group, speed and completion takes priority over spending a great deal of time on detail, as long as the end product works.

As scientists, kinesthetic right-brain people enjoy inventing, doing research and laboratory work, or experimenting in the fields of paleontology, anthropology, quantum physics, or chemistry. If they go into medicine, they may run their own practices so they can have the freedom to set their own hours, or move from one patient to another in ten different rooms.

They may be involved in sports fields, as athletes, coaches, instructors, trainers, or owning a sports facility or team. They may be involved with dancing, gymnastics, golf, track, skiing, skating, swimming, sailing, snorkeling, surfing, biking, gymnastics, horseback riding, Rollerblading, karate, judo, horseback riding, or aerobics, and so on. They may play football, soccer, hockey, tennis, and basketball for fun, but may have to work harder to adjusting to being on an organized professional team because of the rigors of the schedule, discipline, and routine involved in that lifestyle.

They may enjoy the adventure and risks involved in police work, fire fighting, the space program, or the Army, Navy, Marines, or Coast Guard. Many of them like to be self-employed so they do not have to follow someone else's schedule. They may run their own computer, construction, painting, wallpapering, cleaning, moving, lawn, maintenance, plumbing, electrical, or repair companies.

They can be involved in building, making, or fixing things such as cars, houses, boats, motorcycles, computers, appliances, machines, or furniture. They may do work that requires physical exertion such as construction, building bridges, or lifting boxes. Some work in jobs that require traveling, but with little talk. Long-distance driving, flying, chauffeuring, making deliveries, and trucking may satisfy their need to move, if they are not constrained by time schedules.

Kinesthetic right-brain writers write short action stories that get to the point or how-to books that give key points without much detail. If they are artists, they like art requiring action—huge canvasses or sculptures with strong movement of color and design. They tend to make quick, impressionistic drawings that give a general idea of what they are trying to say. If they are actors or actresses, they may prefer parts with less talk and more action or be stunt people. If they are musicians, they enjoy playing instruments in which they can move their body. If they are singers, they prefer doing so with movement or dance. Kinesthetic right-brain learners tend to be better at playing by ear rather than reading notes.

They also tend to be imaginative and can come up with new tunes or forms of music.

Their imagination, new ideas, openness to change, and inventiveness make them an excellent resource. Their commitment to "doing" makes them product oriented and able to produce a large amount of work in a short amount of time. As they move, the world also moves forward into new avenues and directions.

Adapting Learning to a Kinesthetic Right-Brain Style
Kinesthetic right-brain learners need to ask instructor to provide the big picture or overview using short, sensory language and let them do kinesthetic activities in a global, creative, free-flowing way. Since it is hard for kinesthetic right-brain learners to follow auditory presentations, they need a written copy of the notes or readings or take dictation of a lecture and convert each word into: a) a movie in their mind in which they imagine and feel themselves acting out the parts; b) a drawing they make with key words or numbers in colorful, artistic, and creative ways, while standing up at a white board or flip chart and writing with their large arm muscles; c) a mind map in color in which they show the main topic, the details, and their interconnections; or d) a kinesthetic project. They may need to find corresponding pictures, movies, or activities, in which they can participate in real-life demonstrations. They can convert information into a mind map that gives the big picture of the subject they are learning.

CHAPTER 4: CHOOSING THE BEST INSTRUCTION, MATERIALS, AND LEARNING ENVIRONMENT TO IMPROVE MEMORY, READING AND LISTENING COMPREHENSION, NOTE TAKING, STUDY SKILLS, AND TEST-TAKING SKILLS TO ACCELERATE LEARNING

Once we understand the characteristics of one's Superlink and learning style and brain style, we can choose the best instruction, materials and learning environment to improve memory, reading and listening comprehension, study, note taking, and test-taking skills. You will discover:

- how instruction should be delivered to fit the learner's superlink learning style and brain style.
- the learning materials you should use for the learner's unique superlink.
- the learning environment the learner needs for his/her brain's fastest superlink.
- how to convert information from the learner's weaker superlink learning style to their best style.

As the instructor or coordinator choose the type of instruction, learning materials, and learning environment that will allow the learner to absorb information that matches their superlink learning style in order to learn quickly.

Fit the Instruction and Materials to the Learner's Superlink Learning Style and Brain Style

There are many ways to learn a subject. The medium of instruction and the materials are the communication methods used to convey the material. Below are some of the different instructional media and materials.

Written material: Books, eBooks, digital downloads, PDFs, textbooks, manuals, guidebooks, booklets, pamphlets, reference materials such as encyclopedias, almanacs, dictionaries, thesauruses, magazines, journals, newspaper, microfilm, microfiche, scripts, screenplays, poetry, charts, lists, diagrams, graphs, faxed material, emails, blogs, ezine articles, Internet postings, websites, etc.

Graphic material: Photographs, illustrations, pictures, drawings, maps, atlases, posters, cartoons, diagrams and charts with graphics, digital graphic downloads, graphic eBooks, PDFs, websites with graphics, illustrated apps, etc.

Audio-Visual Material: Apps, digital audio downloads, streaming audio over the Internet, audiotapes, CDs, slides, power-point, filmstrips, DVDs, streaming videos, 3-D movies, radio, television, distance learning through teleconferencing, web conferences, web meetings, and webinars, cable television, educational television, and public broadcasting.

From Computers: Information from the Internet, streaming video and audio, software programs, apps, virtual reality, webinars, web conferences, telesemimars, social media, e-mail, distance learning via computer, and on-line courses and degrees programs.

Hands-on Activities: Writing, typing, drawing, sketching, painting, creating graphics on the computer, sculpture, building, constructing, arts and crafts, using tools, machinery or equipment, role-playing, simulations, learning games, using manipulatives, dramatization, film-making, video production, theater productions, music productions, demonstrations, making discoveries, exploration, performing experiments, sports, exercises, etc.

Real-life Experiences: On-the-job training, fieldwork, trips to museums, learning centers (such as oceanariums, seaquariums, forest preserves, or environmental centers), or engaging in apprenticeships in stores or retail businesses, service industries, construction sites, hospitals, schools, factories, farms, delivery companies, airports, shipyards, railway stations, banks, the stock exchange, supermarkets, auto repair shops, art studios, theater or dance companies, concert halls, etc.), playing on sports teams (football, baseball, basketball, soccer, hockey, golf, etc.), or engage in training programs coordinated between places of employment and schools, etc.

Personal Instructors: Direct instruction from teachers, professors, instructors, guides, mentors, life coaches, athletic or sports coaches, certified personal trainers, facilitators, trainers, skilled craftspeople, employers, managers or supervisors. (The person may instruct through oral presentations or lectures, reading aloud material to the students or requiring students to read it themselves, providing printed graphic material, audio-visual material, and computer technology, setting up hands-on learning activities, or putting the learners into real-life situations in order to learn.)

Combinations of the above: Any of the above teaching methods can be combined.

Based on the description of the learner's superlink, choose the instructional medium and materials from the above lists that corresponds with the learner's Superlinks learning style and brain style. For example, if he/she is a visual right-brain person, the medium and materials needed would be graphic material, movies, videos, printed material written in a visual right-brain style, or real life experiences.

As the instructor or coordinator of a student's learning, set it up in the way that will help him/her learn quickly. You can help the student by choosing the best medium or learning material, or selecting the learning environment. Convert any instruction into the learner's best learning style. The following pages show you the instructional media compatible with the different learning styles and how to convert medium not in the learner's style into their best superlink. Think of it as a translation system to show you what can be done do to turn a poor situation into an optimal one.

The following information will enable the instructor/coordinator to convert a medium of instruction and materials or some aspect of them into the best medium of instruction and materials for the learner's superlink.

The reason more than just Kinesthetic left-brain and Kinesthetic right-brain information is provided is that learners of any learning style and brain style can exhibit characteristics of ADHD or ADD when the instruction materials and environment do not match how they learn best.

Converting Instruction and Materials into the Learner's Superlink Learning Style and Brain Style to Improve Memory, Reading and Listening Comprehension, Study Skills, Note Taking, and Test-Taking Skills

Superlink: Visual Left-Brain Learners:
Media Type:
Written Material: Ideal for visual left-brain learners
Graphic Material: Label and describe graphic material.

Audio-Visual Material: Use a corresponding study guide or transcript or take notes to review later.
Computers: When graphics are the only displayed media, search for a corresponding online manual to read that explains the graphics, or have the learner do their own note taking.
Hands-On Activities: Read the directions for the activity or have the learner write their own.
Real-Life Experiences: Refer to a written description of the activity.
Learning from an Instructor: If the presentation is auditory, tactile, or kinesthetic, the learner can make their own outline, directions or study guide to read and comprehend later.

Superlink: Visual Right-Brain Learners:
Media Type:
Written Material: Draw pictures or diagrams to accompany the text.
Graphic Material: This is ideal for visual right-brain learners.
Audio-Visual Material: For written text, or audio media without graphics, have the learner create their own sketches or graphic materials in color.
Computers: For programs with written text, the learner can draw their own illustrations, graphic images, or mind maps to accompany the text.
Hands-On Activities: Make an illustrated instruction booklet for the activity.
Real-Life Experiences: Take notes in color on the experience and illustrate them.
Learning from an Instructor: If the instruction is auditory, tactile, or kinesthetic, take notes by drawing sketches or graphic images of the material in color.

<u>Superlink: Auditory Left-Brain Learners:</u>
<u>Media Type:</u>

Written Material: Read the material aloud and discuss it.

Graphic Material: Have the learner talk about the material aloud or discuss it with others.

Audio-Visual Material: Ideal for auditory left-brain learners. For visual media without sound, talk about the material aloud to himself/herself or discuss with others.

Computers: Read aloud any text that appears on the screen or discuss it with others.

Hands-On Activities: Talk about the activities while doing them or create their own auditory step-by-step directions.

Real-Life Experiences: Talk about the activities while doing them or create their own auditory step-by-step directions.

Learning from an Instructor: For a visual, tactile, or kinesthetic presentation, ask questions, discuss, orally describe the process, read aloud what he/she wrote, or verbally describe the moves step-by-step.

<u>Superlink: Auditory Right-Brain Learners:</u>
<u>Media Type:</u>

Written Material: Make an imaginary movie and hear the narration or dialogue spoken with expression, sound effects, or music to accompany the text, or invent rhymes, raps, songs, or rhythmic poetry about the material.

Graphic Material: Create rhymes, raps, songs, mnemonics, or poetry to help remember the material; discuss the material with others, giving the global overview first.

Audio-Visual Material: If visual or auditory material is only the written or spoken word, add sound effects or

read it with expression, while creating songs, rhymes, raps, or mnemonics to go with the material.
Computers: For materials with only written text or the spoken word, add sound effects or music, or read aloud with expression, using entertaining tones of voice.
Hands-On Activities: For visual, tactile, or kinesthetic activities, make a colorful mind map and add sound effects or music, or talk about it with others, using entertaining tones of voice.
Real-Life Experiences: For visual, tactile, or kinesthetic real-life experiences, make a colorful mind map and add sound effects or music, or talk about it with others, using entertaining tones of voice.
Learning from an Instructor: For a visual, tactile, or kinesthetic presentation, have the learner convert it into a movie in their mind, imagining the narration or dialogue with expressive tones of voice, sound effects, and/or music, and/or talk about it with others, using associations, mnemonics, poetry, raps, rhymes, or songs.

Superlink: Tactile Left-Brain Learners:
Media Type:
Written Material: Have the learner copy the material or do note taking in their own hand or type it.
Graphic Material: Have the learner write a description of the graphics in their own hand, type it, do note taking or make a model and label the components.
Audio-Visual Material: Do note taking and/or do the hands-on step-by-step process.
Computers: For graphics, write descriptions in his/her own hand, do note taking or type them out, or do the hands-on step-by-step process.
Hands-On Activities: This is ideal for tactile left-brain learners. Use a step-by-step approach and put it into words.

Real-Life Experiences: For visual, auditory, or kinesthetic activities, do note taking, and involve feelings.
Learning from an Instructor: For visual, auditory, or kinesthetic instruction, do note taking, perform hands-on activities, and involve your feelings.

Superlink: Tactile Right-Brain Learners:
Media Type:
Written Material: Draw, sketch, or make graphics, in color, to illustrate the words.
Graphic Material: Copy or draw the visuals or do a hands-on activity related to it; involving their feelings.
Audio-Visual Material: Draw, sketch, diagram, or make graphics, in color, or do a hands-on activity related to the audio-visual material.
Computers: Convert any written text from computers into graphics. If already in graphic form, copy it by drawing in color.
Hands-On Activities: This is ideal for tactile right-brain learners. Use a global approach beginning with the big picture or overview first.
Real-Life Experiences: Have the learner make color sketches or mind maps with illustrations to remind them of the experience.
Learning from an Instructor: Make sketches or colorful pictorial diagrams or mind maps of the presentation.

Superlink: Kinesthetic Left-Brain Learners:
Media Type:
Written Material: Have the learner act out the words in a step-by-step way or imagine the action in their mind, feeling it in their muscles.
Graphic Material: Have the learner physically act out the graphic representation or imagine the action in their

mind in a step-by-step way, while feeling it in their muscles.

Audio-Visual Material: Have the learner dramatize or imagine acting out the action in their mind, feeling it in their muscles, in a step-by-step way.

Computers: Have the learner physically act out the written text or graphics shown on the computer, or imagine doing the action, while feeling it in their muscles, in a step-by-step way.

Hands-On Activities: Visual, auditory, or tactile activities need to be carried out physically, or have the learner imagine doing the action in their mind, feeling it in their muscles, in a step-by-step way.

Real-Life Experiences: Ideal for kinesthetic left-brain learners. Use as a step-by-step approach and put it into words.

Learning from an Instructor: For visual, auditory, or tactile presentations, the learner can carry them out physically or imagine the action in their mind, feeling it in their muscles, in a step-by-step way, putting in into words.

Superlink: Kinesthetic Right-Brain Learners: Media Type:

Written Material: Have the learner physically act out the words or imagine doing the action in their mind, feeling it in their muscles.

Graphic Material: Have the learner physically act out the graphic representation or imagine doing the action in their mind, feeling it in their muscles.

Audio-Visual Material: Carry out the actions physically or imagine the action in their mind, while feeling it in their muscles.

Computers: Written text or graphics need to be physically carried out, or have the learner imagine the action in their mind, feeling it in their muscles, with freedom of movement and imagination.

Hands-On Activities: For visual, auditory, and tactile activities, have the learner participate in the experience physically or imagine doing the action, feeling it in their muscles, with freedom of movement and imagination.

Real-Life Experiences: This is ideal for kinesthetic right-brain learners. Use a global approach, beginning with the big picture, main idea, or overview.

Learning from an Instructor: For visual, auditory, or tactile instruction, have the learner physically act it out or imagine doing the action in their mind, while feeling it in their muscles, with freedom of movement and imagination.

In summary, each type of instruction and learning material can be made suitable for any type of learner. There is no reason for books and graphic materials to be made only for visual people; books can be produced to appeal to auditory, tactile, and kinesthetic people who are either left-brain or right-brain or both. As a consultant and a writer of learning materials for many years, I have developed programs that deliver instruction through the medium that matches the learners' best superlink learning style and brain style. For example, I created an entire pre-K, K-12, college and adult reading program, called Keys to Reading Success and Superlinks to Accelerated Learning with lessons in all eight superlink styles so everyone can excel in reading, reading and listening comprehension, vocabulary, phonics, fluency, memory, note taking, study skills, and test-taking skills. Any medium can be converted to match the learner's style.

Exercise: Use the above information to find the best media of instruction and materials that matches the learner's superlink learning style. Take notes of all the instructional methods and media materials that match their best learning style and brain style to improve memory and reading and listening comprehension. Remember, if the learner is a combination of superlinks, select media materials from different parts of the above information, since they have two or more best superlink learning styles and brain styles combinations.

The Learning Environment the Learner Needs

The learning environment refers to where the learner will work, read, or study: the conditions in the room and other stimuli that can enhance or inhibit their ability to learn. You may have set them up with the right delivery of instruction and the right materials, but if their environment causes them discomfort or distractions it will be harder to concentrate. To improve memory, reading and listening comprehension, study skills, note taking, and test-taking skills to accelerate learning you want to eliminate as many steps that block their progress as possible.

Below is a list summarizing the best learning environment to improve memory, reading comprehension, listening comprehension, study skills, note taking, and test-taking skills for each superlink, followed by coping skills for adapting a noncompatible environment into one that is compatible for the learner.

Superlink: Visual Left-Brain Learners:
Best Learning Environment:

Written material and the speaker are clearly visible.
No visual clutter or disorganization.
Printed material is neat and free of errors.
Can work with or without music or auditory distractions because they can tune it out.
Room is complete with filing systems, visual organizers, time schedules, calendars, and clocks.

The instructor arrives on times and finishes on time.

Coping Strategies to Adapt a Noncompatible Environment:

Try to sit close to the front to see posted visual materials.
Keep their own area neat and organized.
The learner can help clean up, organize, and decorate the rest of the room.
Correct errors in printed material.
Request a time schedule.
Wear a watch.
Offer to be a timekeeper.

Superlink: Visual Right-Brain Learners

Best Learning Environment:

Graphic or written material and the speaker are clearly visible.
Visually attractive, colorful, and creative environments.
Can work with or without music or auditory distractions because they can tune it out.
Flexible schedule allows the learner to come and go at varying times.

Coping Strategies to Adapt a Noncompatible Environment:

Sit near the front to see posted visual graphic materials.
Keep their own area colorful, well designed, and attractive.
Learner can help decorate the area of the room at which they have to look.
Use a color-coded, decorative calendar to artistically track their deadlines. Put up sticky-note messages to attract their attention and remind them of deadlines and due dates.

Superlink: Auditory Left-Brain Learners:

Best Learning Environment:

They can listen to others and discuss their own ideas.

Only one auditory stimulus at a time.
No music in the background while studying or reading.
Silence for reading or studying.
Orderly environment has filing systems, organizers, and time schedules.
Instructor gives out schedules. Comes on time and finishes on time.

Coping Strategies to Adapt a Noncompatible Environment:

Sit with someone who will discuss the topic with them.
Sit where they can hear the speaker well.
Stay away from areas with noise distraction.
Bring headphones or earplugs to tune out music or distracting sounds when reading or studying.
If they need to talk to themselves or read aloud, sit in an area where they will not disturb others. (Most likely the only ones who will be disturbed are other auditory people.)
Ask for a time schedule. Wear a watch. Offer to be a timekeeper.

Superlink: Auditory Right-Brain Learners:

Best Learning Environment:

The sounds in the environment are pleasant.
Sounds are harmonious with one another, for example, music combined with natural sounds.
Talk is kept to a minimum, with key points emphasized.
Flexible time schedule.
Speaker is clearly audible and speaks with good expression.
Absolute quiet for studying.
No music in the background while studying or reading.

Coping Strategies to Adapt a Noncompatible Environment:

Listen to music while doing work that does not require abstract thinking in the form of words.

Sit where they can hear the speaker clearly.
Avoid areas with noise distraction.
Sit with someone who can repeat key points and verbal directions slowly and repeatedly, if needed, until they understand them.
Bring headphones or earplugs to tune out distractions.
If they need to talk to themselves, read aloud, or make their own sound effects, sit in an area where they will not disturb others. (Most likely the only ones who will be disturbed are other auditory people.)

Superlink: Tactile Left-Brain Learners:
Best Learning Environment:
Environment is physically and emotionally comfortable.
They can sit next to people they like.
They know the schedule and a clock is available.
Room is organized and neat, where they can easily grab what they need.
They are permitted to write, draw, and doodle as they listen or read.
Can work or without music they like.
Instructor has a positive communication style, using praise and positive words and positive nonverbal communication.
Coping Strategies to Adapt a Noncompatible Environment:
Sit in a comfortable seat or bring a cushion or pillow to make uncomfortable seats feel better.
If they do not like air-conditioning or heat, sit far from the ventilators or blowers. If they do not like sun glare, avoid sitting in the linc of sunlight. If they like sun, or need a view of greenery or a peaceful setting, sit near the window.
Select a location where they feel emotionally comfortable. Sit near people they like.
Ask for a time schedule. Wear a watch.

Keep an organizer for their papers.
Keep notepaper and pens available. Sit where doodling, writing, or touching objects does not bother the instructor or others.
If they need music they like to work, bring headphones so as not to disturb others.

Superlink: Tactile Right-Brain Learners:
Best Learning Environment:
Use comfortable seats. (Some may like to stretch out on the floor or couch, sit on a desktop, or recline or stretch out in their seats.)
Physically and emotionally comfortable environment.
They can sit near people they like and stay far away from people who they think do not like them.
They are allowed to doodle, draw, or sketch.
They can work with or without music, but it needs to be music they like.
Flexible schedule.
Instructor is someone they like and admire.
Coping Strategies to Adapt a Noncompatible Environment:
Select their own seating to be physically or emotionally comfortable. Bring a pillow or cushion if the seat is uncomfortable.
If they like scenery, sit near a window. Sit near or away from heaters, air-conditioners or sun-glare, if that makes them uncomfortable, depending on their comfort level.
Sit near someone they like. Avoid sitting near people who make them feel uncomfortable or upset.
Keep drawing paper, colored pens, or markers for doodling and sketching, and sit where this does not distract others.
If they like music to keep them feeling relaxed and positive, bring headphones so as to listen and not disturb others.

Keep a color-coded calendar or use sticky-notes as reminder of time.
Keep objects or belongings that make them feel good to touch on their desk or table. Give their desk or area a personal touch.

Superlink: Kinesthetic Left-Brain Learners:
Best Learning Environment:
Plenty of space to stretch out and move around.
They can get out of their seat or work standing up.
Comfortable seats.
White boards or flip charts allow them to stand up and write.
Neat, organized surroundings.
Time schedules.
Coping Strategies to Adapt a Noncompatible Environment:
Sit near the back of the room so they can move around without distracting anyone.
If they have to sit to work, use a chair in which they can lean back, stretch out, wiggle, or move a lot.
Ask for a time schedule. Wear a watch.
Bring a challenging game or activity or something to do quietly at their seat if they get bored after finishing work earlier than others and have to wait for the next part of the lesson.
If they like music, bring headphones so as not to disturb others.
Do arm or leg exercises at their seat if they get bored or restless.
When studying, stay in a study carrel or put up a book or divider to block out the distraction of others' movements, or face a wall.

Superlink: Kinesthetic Right-Brain Learners:

Best Learning Environment:

Enough space to move around and stretch out.
They can get out of their seat or work standing up.
Room has comfortable places to stretch out on the floor or couch, and if sitting is required, use chairs on which they can lean back, stretch their legs, wiggle, or move.
They can play learning or movement games.
They are permitted to work with or without music.
When studying, sit at a study carrel or have a divider to block out the view of others' movements and activities.
White boards, flip charts, or smart boards allow them to stand up and write.
Flexible time schedule, and if work is done, allowed to leave early or keep working, if they want, well past the finishing time.
Competitions, rewards, and awards for achieving a goal.

Coping Strategies to Adapt to a Noncompatible Environment:

Select a place where they can move around without disturbing others, preferably at the back of the room.
Make sure if they have to sit, the seat allows them to lean back, stretch their legs, wiggle and move around.
Bring a challenging game or activity, or something to do quietly when bored while waiting for the next task if they finish before the others.
If they like music while learning, listen using headphones so as not to disturb others.
Work at a study carrel or use a book or divider to block out distractions from others' movements or actions.
Keep a color-coded calendar or use sticky-notes as reminders of time schedules.

Exercise: Use some of the above suggestions for the learner's superlink learning style and brain style and apply them to learning any subject quickly.

CHAPTER 5: HOW TO LEARN TO IMPROVE AND INCREASE READING COMPREHENSION AND LISTENING COMPREHENSION USING THE BEST SUPERLINK LEARNING STYLE AND BRAIN STYLE

Once information is received in the fastest, most natural manner through the learner's superlink, the next step is to improve reading comprehension and listening comprehension to ensure that the learner understands or comprehends the material. Think of it as having a delivery person get past the checkpoints in a high-security building. Using the best and fastest route, the letter is delivered. The next question is, "Do you understand what the message says?" Understanding the message when the learner reads is called "reading comprehension." Grasping the message when the learner listens is called "listening comprehension."

We may have material conveyed to us through our best learning style, but without training, we still may not comprehend it, or we may comprehend only a portion of it. Comprehension, for either reading or listening, is a skill that can be learned. Think back to a test the learner may not have done well on, painful as the memory may be. Did he/she study hard only to score seventy-five percent, eighty-eight percent, or even way below sixty-five percent? What happened? They only comprehended a portion of the material they learned. They thought they studied hard. What was missing? The learner may not have learned the skill of reading or listening comprehension.

In many schools today, teachers continue to test students' reading comprehension and listening comprehension. The latest emphasis in schools is on "close reading," where we read to gather and refer back to information in the text. How can a student do this without being taught how to comprehend? If they fail, teachers have them study again, retest them, and see what they score the second or third time around. Yet are they ever taught *how* to comprehend? We often think that reading comprehension or listening comprehension are genetically-transmitted traits with which we are born or which we pick up by osmosis. It is not. Reading comprehension and listening comprehension are learned, acquired skills. In this chapter, the instructor/coordinator will learn the secrets to increasing the learner's reading comprehension and listening comprehension, and hopefully it will not remain secret anymore to the learner. From kindergarten and first grade up to college and at the adult level, everyone needs to learn how to comprehend, but many adults never learned reading or listening comprehension at all. So get ready for Reading and Listening Comprehension Made Easy 101!

Reading and Listening Comprehension Techniques for the Kinesthetic Left and Right-Brain Superlinks

By now you have an idea that people with different learning styles and brain hemispheric preferences think differently, remember differently, and respond to the world in a different way. They also comprehend in a different manner. The following are reading comprehension techniques I have developed and used successfully with people of Kinesthetic left and right-brain learning styles and brain hemispheric preferences. If you use these techniques with the learner, comprehension can improve drastically. Many people who were previously struggling with comprehension have become so successful through the use of these techniques that they can actually comprehend and remember one hundred percent of what they read. If this were taught in schools, even from kindergarten and first grade on, we would see higher comprehension achievement scores for all students and adults. For those who are good readers, they may already intuitively know how to comprehend everything they read. But there are millions of students and adults who struggle with reading. They may pick up the gist of what they read, but miss most of it. The exercise in this section is designed to sharpen their reading comprehension whether they are a good reader or they are one of the millions of adults who managed to make it through school—or even through graduate school—but who wished they had known a way to read better and comprehend more fully. Many adults who have successful careers are still not satisfied with their ability to fully comprehend and remember what they read. They feel they have to take a long time to make it through readings and have no memory of what they read. Overwhelmed by the many professional journals or training materials they are required to read at the workplace, they are too embarrassed to tell anyone about their struggle or to seek help. With changes in the workplace where innovations require people to learn new skills for their current jobs, or with frequent job loss due to companies going out of business or downsizing, people must look for new jobs, which may require learning and comprehending an entirely new career. In addition, with an ever-increasing average life span, people are living well into their senior years and want to keep learning. With the current emphasis on keeping their brain and memory sharp, seniors in great numbers are engaged in ongoing learning, so these tools can help them continue to keep their brain active. This chapter provides some tools to make reading easier for those who want to learn more quickly and easily but who have been previously slowed down by poor comprehension techniques.

The basic technique for reading comprehension, which I have named "experiential" or "virtual reality" comprehension, are described below, followed by adaptations for the kinesthetic superlinks learning styles.

Instructions for Reading a Passage to Improve Reading Comprehension: To begin this exercise, the learner will read a sample passage, phrase by phrase. They are going to imagine that they are a movie director and are going to convert the words into a movie or video. Their job is to set up the scene, guide the actors and actresses as to what they should be doing and what their facial expressions should be, control the sound, and direct the action. Pretend that the printed text is a screenplay they have to convert back into action. Did they ever realize that printed text is merely a transcription of imaginary or real-life events that have been converted into words so that those who were not on the spot could read it to find out what happened? Reading is converting words back into the actual experiences or ideas that the author is trying to convey. That is their job as an imaginary movie director—convert the words back into a movie. The following adaptations will be made by people with each superlink learning style. I have given each type of reading a name so we can refer back to them.

Kinesthetic Experiential Reading Comprehension—Left and Right-Brain: As the learner reads, they will imagine themselves experiencing the action or doing the movement described in the movie. They need to become the actors or actresses and carry out the movements themselves. Make the movie come alive—at a physical level. The question to ask themselves after reading each phrase or sentence is: "What am I *doing* or *experiencing* in my movie?" Turn everything into an action that can be experienced in their muscles.

Kinesthetic left-brain people will be more attuned to the actions along with a verbal description of the action.

Kinesthetic right-brain people will act out the movie in their mind. They will convert everything into some movement that they can feel their muscles make, without needing long verbal description. Only a few action words are needed.

Now let's learn how to use the experiential or virtual reality reading comprehension technique. Below is a sample reading passage, but *do not* read it until instructed to do so. For the moment skip down to below the passage and read it according to the "How to Read the Sample Passage: 'Rapid Learning.'" This exercise will teach the learner how to read using full "experiential comprehension" or "virtual reality reading comprehension."

Sample Passage: "Rapid Learning"

An eager young man desired a part-time job to help make his way through Stanford University. As he stood before Louis Janin one Friday morning, he was told there was only a stenographer position available.

"I'd love it!" exclaimed the excited young man. "However, I can't start until next Wednesday."

Bright and early on Wednesday morning, the young man reported for duty.

"I like the promptness and enthusiasm," Janin assured the lad. "I do have one question. Why couldn't you start on Monday?"

"Well, you see, sir, I had to find a typewriter and learn how to use it," replied the young man—Herbert

Hoover—who would later become president of the United States.

How to Read the Sample Passage Called "Rapid Learning"

Read the first few words of the above passage, "An eager young man." Either with eyes opened or closed, ask the learner one of the following questions according to their superlink learning style:

Kinesthetic Learner: "What action or movement is the learner (or the characters) experiencing their muscles doing in their movie now?"

Think of this as the opening scene of the movie. The first thing that will appear on the screen is "an eager young man." Since they are the director, imagine a young man in their mind, any way they want, to begin with. Do not read ahead yet, but work with that one phrase. (Note: As they continue reading, the passage may describe him more specifically, which at that time they will then move to the next scene and alter that man to fit the new information provided in the text.) Some of them may imagine a tall man, a thin man, and so forth. Unless, and until, the passage describes the man further, they can imagine him any way they wish. It is helpful to populate the movie with people they already know, such as family, friends, co-workers, or famous personalities, such as athletes, movie stars, or performers, etc. How they imagine that man is based on their superlink learning style. If they are kinesthetic, they will imagine him in motion, and feel that movement in their muscles as if they were moving. Instead of a stationary man just standing there, a kinesthetic learner should imagine him bursting on the screen in motion, such as running, swimming, playing sports, driving a car, or anything involving large muscle movement.

Next, let's work on the word "eager." As director, have the actor in the movie express eagerness according to their superlink learning style. For example, a visual learner should see the man showing an expression of eagerness of his face. An auditory learner should hear eagerness in his voice, or have him say something to express eagerness. A tactile learner should feel eagerness within himself or herself to identify with the character's emotion. A kinesthetic learner should act out something that relates to being eager, such as excitedly opening a wrapped birthday gift, eager to find out what it contains, or being pumped up about winning a football game.

Now, read the next group of words: "desired a part-time job to make his way through Stanford University." Based on their superlink learning style they will ask themselves one of the following questions, "What am I seeing (hearing or saying, feeling or touching, or what action am I doing or experiencing) on my movie screen now?" Then describe to themselves as director what they want to appear on the screen to make that phrase come alive in their superlink style. Kinesthetic learners may experience hopping in their car to drive to a part-time job, racing through the streets, feeling the sensation of steering the car and the twists and turns of the road as they sway from side to side. It's their movie. They have the basic words to work with, but since they mean different things to different people, their movie is totally theirs. The author may have had one thing in mind, but when it is not fully described, then some portion is left to the reader's imagination.

Suppose it is important for the learner to recall the words "Stanford University," because that information is needed for a test they must take or information they must talk about at their job. If they are familiar with the college, then based on their superlink learning and brain style, see it, hear the sounds on campus, feel themselves as part of the student body, or perform an action such as playing on its sports team or doing a science experiment in one of its labs. If they are not familiar with this particular school, find an association that they already have in their mind that sounds like or is spelled like Stanford. Do they know a person by the name of Stan whom they can visualize? Or think of smaller words that are a part of a whole word, such as *stand* and *Ford*. If they are kinesthetic, they can feel themselves standing next to the Ford, and then jumping in and driving it away. There are times when these small details may not be important, such as when they are reading for pleasure, but when they are going to be held accountable for what they read, these associations will help them retain the information long after they close the book. Doing this exercise with detailed information will sharpen their brain and memory to comprehend better what they are reading at the moment, as well as develop neural pathways and more automaticity for improving reading comprehension for anything they read in the future.

Go on to the read the next group of words: "As he stood before Louis Janin…" Again, the learner should ask himself/herself, based on their superlink learning and brain style, "What am I seeing (hearing or saying, feeling or touching, or what action am I doing or experiencing) on my movie screen now?" As director, continue rolling their movie cameras along. Without any description of the man, Louis Janin, it is up to each reader to imagine what he is like in his or her own superlink learning style. Kinesthetic learners should have him do something in which his large motor muscles are in motion, and then feel themselves doing that same action within their own muscles, for example, running into the office. Again, to remember his name, think of a Louis they know personally, a famous personality, or someone from history by that name and imagine him in their movie. Janin may not ring a bell with them, so associate it with some similar-looking or –sounding word: Jan, Jani, Jan "in" a place. Insert the association, imagined in their own superlink learning style, into their movie as a flashback, thought bubble as in a cartoon, or cutaway to help them remember the person's name.

Take the next group of words, "one Friday morning…" Note that if there are a variety of images, he/she can sometimes break a sentence into phrases, but sometimes they can work with a whole sentence. The benefit of breaking a sentence up in the beginning stages of mastering this technique is that sometimes, when the sentence has too much going on in it, they tend to visualize only a part of it, skipping over some images. Until they get used to this technique, imagine every word of the text. They will discover for themselves how much they can read at a time so they do not miss anything. Back to the words in the sample text, "one Friday morning." What comes on their movie screen when they think of Friday morning? The kinesthetics may be passing out tickets that they picked up for the friends at the office for a basketball game for the next day.

Next, the passage reads: "…he was told there was only a stenographer position available." Go ahead and experience that in his/her own sensory modality on their movie screen. Based on their superlink learning style, they can see a stenographer at work, hear the sound of someone hitting the keys, feel the sensation of their fingers on the keys, or feel their arm movements as they strike the keys. Suppose they do not know what a stenographer is. What happens to their movie? As director, the actors and actresses are waiting around for them to "direct' them to act out the scene. Without their knowing what a stenographer is, what happens to their movie? It stops. This means that to keep the movie rolling so there is no gap in their comprehension, they need to find the definition of the word, act it out according to their superlink learning style (either seeing it, hearing it, feeling or touching something related to it, or doing an action) and inserting that back into the movie. Many gaps in their comprehension is caused by not knowing a word, skipping it, and wondering why they cannot remember totally what they read. To be prepared for such circumstances, they can use any of the following tools: use a dictionary, either a physical book or a dictionary on the Internet, ask someone, or use the feature in some of the eBook readers that allow you to highlight a word so the definition pops up. Finding the meaning of unknown words will help their comprehension of what they are currently reading and build their vocabulary so that the next time the word appears in text or conversation, they already have a movie image for it.

The story continues: "'I'd love it!' exclaimed the excited young man." Although this is an auditory scene, the kinesthetic learners may experience themselves jumping up or hitting their fist into the air with a loud "Yes!"

The passage next reads, "However, I can't start until next Wednesday." The learner should ask themselves what they see (or hear or say, feel or touch, or what actions they experience doing) on their movie screen next. Are the kinesthetics remembering Wednesday because it is the day they go to fitness class?

Have the learner read the rest of the paragraph by themselves, breaking it up as follows between the slashes: "Bright and early on Wednesday morning/ the young man reported for duty./ 'I like the promptness and enthusiasm,' Janin assured the lad./ 'I do have one question. Why couldn't you start on Monday?'/ 'Well, you see, sir, I had to find a typewriter and learn how to use it,'/ replied the young man—Herbert Hoover/—who would later become president of the United States."

As they read each of the above phrases, remember the question to ask themselves that applies to their kinesthetic superlink learning style. Remember, they will have to be thinking the question to themselves as they read without anyone else reminding them. The question is: "What action am I experiencing and doing on my movie screen now?" With practice, they will no longer need to ask this question in their mind; they will just automatically convert the words into the movie. They should not skip anything, because they will find that what they did not imagine in their mind may be lost even minutes after they read it. What they do imagine in their superlink learning style will be there long after they read the passage.

Now, the learner needs to prove to themselves how much of the passage they remember. They will answer the following questions about "their movie." While they reply, give only the basic answer that appeared in the *printed* story and leave out the additional information they created and added to help them remember. Answer purely from memory without looking at the passage again. No peeking back!

Questions:

1) Who is this story about?
2) What was he looking for?
3) To what school did he go?
4) What day did he have the interview?
5) What part of the day did he have the interview?
6) Who interviewed him?
7) What position was available?
8) How did he feel about taking the position that was available?
9) What day did he want to start?

10) Why did he choose that day to start work?

Answers: (Note, they may have added the description they made in their mind to the answers, but the basic answers are below:

1) Possible answers: a young man, an eager young man, or Herbert Hoover
2) A part-time job, or a part-time job to help him through school
3) Stanford University
4) Friday
5) Morning
6) Louis Janin, or a man
7) Stenographer
8) He was excited, or he said, "I'd love it."
9) Wednesday
10) He needed time to learn how to type.

The key to experiential reading comprehension is to visualize the passage as vividly as he/she can, using their best learning style. When they visualize and make it real, their brain is taking it in as if it were actually happening to them. They tend to remember events that seem real to them better than they remember those they read about. Think of how real a dream seems. It is not really happening, but while we are experiencing it, it feels real to us. Those who can recall their dreams find that they can remember them as clearly as events in their lives. We can use that same mental ability to help us remember what we read for the purpose of learning. If we experience the passage as if it were really happening to us, we will comprehend and remember it better. The kinesthetic learners will feel as if they really did it. It is startling to see how people who were previously scoring anywhere from a D or F on comprehension tests in a wide variety of subjects, began to score an A when they used this method. They learned how to achieve total comprehension of whatever they read. Others, marveling at their friend's new "ability" often wanted to learn it, too. The beauty of the method is that it can be learned by anyone of any age.

Did you ever wonder how a teenager who loves sports can study for hours for a test and come home with a low grade, yet can rattle off every sports statistic of his or her favorite team or all the players and give you a detailed description of each of their games? Does he or she have a comprehension problem? Certainly not, as evidenced by his or her seemingly fantastic comprehension when it comes to sports. It is just that this material—action sports—may be compatible with his or her superlink learning style and brain style, while the material he or she is studying is not action-oriented. But anything can be converted to a medium he or she will understand. If the material were converted into action, then the learner would remember it as vividly as the sports event.

This method can work with *any* reading material, both fiction and nonfiction, such as information reading. The key is to convert anything they read into a video, DVD, or movie. Think about how many scientific documentaries they have seen on television. They even make movies, DVDs, and videos about math, language, history, and computers! When they read in these various content areas all they are doing is becoming the producer or director and making a movie out of the material. They can even do this with abstract subjects that do not even seem to have any action. We will now see how to use experiential reading with a technical passage provided below. The same technique can be used for reading texts in science, math, social studies, technology, and content that is not about people or action. The learner should not read the passage until he/she has been given instructions in the directions below the passage called: "How to Read the Sample Technical Nonfiction Passage: 'Photosynthesis.'"

Sample Technical Nonfiction Passage: "Photosynthesis"

Photosynthesis is a biochemical reaction that occurs when a green plant takes in sunlight, carbon dioxide from the air, and water, and converts them using its chlorophyll to carbohydrates and oxygen.

How to Read the Sample Nonfiction Technical Passage: "Photosynthesis"

Start with the first phrase: "Photosynthesis is a biochemical reaction that occurs when a green plant…" If the learner knows what photosynthesis is, ask themselves, "How can I represent this on my movie screen so viewers will know what it is? What am I seeing (hearing or saying, feeling, or doing?)". If they do not know what photosynthesis is, the passage cues them by saying "a biochemical reaction" which lets them know that the rest of the sentence will tell them what it is. If they first need to read the whole sentence to picture photosynthesis, then do so, or look it up in a dictionary. On their movie screen, the kinesthetic learners may experience themselves digging in the garden.

Let's read on: "takes in sunlight." What is happening in their movie now? The kinesthetic learners may fly from the sun down to the plant.

Next it says, "carbon dioxide from the air." How will they portray carbon dioxide on their movie screen? The kinesthetic learners may imagine themselves writing, while standing up, the symbol "CO_2" with their arm tracing it in the air or writing on a flip chart, or experience themselves bouncing around in the air, knocking into many other molecules, and then being forcefully sucked into the plant.

The reading continues: "and water." What is on their movie screen now? The kinesthetic learners may experience themselves surfing the waves in the ocean. Whatever it takes to remember what they read is fair game.

Next, it says: "and converts them using its chlorophyll." Again, they may or may not know what chlorophyll is. If they don't know, what happens to their movie? They cannot make an image for that scene and now have a gap in their movie. The viewers are suddenly lost because the screen went blank. This shows what happens when they skip over vocabulary words they do not know. There is suddenly a gap in their understanding. At this point, what they need to do is to look up the word. Get a dictionary, use a glossary in the text or look it up on an online dictionary on the Internet to find out, on the spot, what it is. If they wait, they may forget to look it up, and when they look it up later it is out of context and will not be as meaningful. If they stop and look up an unknown vocabulary word at the point that it enters the scene in the movie, they will remember it because they actively "directed it" in their movie, and then it makes sense in the context. Let us look up "chlorophyll" first, so they can proceed with the movie. They look in a glossary and find that chlorophyll is green material in the tissues of plants used for photosynthesis. Now back to their movie. The kinesthetic learners may experience themselves sucking in the carbon dioxide and water, and when the sun bombards them, shaking them at high speed to convert them.

Next, they read: "into carbohydrates." How will they portray carbohydrates in their movie now? The kinesthetics learners may feel themselves eating some carbohydrates as they rush out to the gym to exercise.

Finally, they conclude the passage by reading: "and oxygen." How will they show that in their movie to viewers in the audience? The kinesthetic learners may be running on the track and taking in deep gulps of oxygen, feeling the muscles of their chest expand as they breathe in.

Now, let's do a reading comprehension practice test on this passage. Answer without looking back at the passage. As a question comes up, relax and recall the movie he/she created. Do not try to force themselves to remember the words—just let the images come up. Kinesthetic learners, "What did I do?"

1) What is this passage about?
2) What do green plants do?
3) What does the green plant need for the process of photosynthesis to take place?
4) What does chlorophyll do?
5) What two things do green plants give off after chlorophyll converts the ingredients it took in?

Answers: 1) photosynthesis (or the description of photosynthesis); 2) take in sunlight, carbon dioxide from the air, and water and converts them using its chlorophyll to carbohydrates and oxygen; 3) chlorophyll (or sunlight, carbon dioxide and water); 4) convert sunlight, carbon dioxide, and water into oxygen and carbohydrates; 5) oxygen and carbohydrates.

They can see how this process works well with technical material. Anything can be converted into a movie, and they will remember it much better because the reading material becomes an activity they experienced through their best learning style.

They may also understand from the above example why they have to read a passage in small parts.

Remember, whatever they do not portray in their movie may be forgotten. Technical reading requires more careful attention than pleasure reading. Since there are so many technical details, they need to take the time to image everything. If they do not, they may take double, triple, or quadruple the time to learn by reading this passage over and over in the hopes that they will remember each detail. But by experiencing it as a movie or as live action, they can recall it with even one careful or close reading.

They may say that this feels like it is taking them longer to read. First of all, this was a demonstration to teach them how to do it, so you were "talking them" through the process. They will be asking the question in their own mind, which is faster. After practicing for a few days or weeks they will not need to verbalize the question anymore; they will automatically convert the words into images. Think of it as taking a bite of food, chewing, and swallowing—they take a bite of the word, digest it, and get the image. The process of reading a word and getting an image will not be two separate occurrences; they will happen simultaneously. They will reach a point when they read the word and the images appear immediately, and they can clip along at a fast pace, getting a series of images without even being aware of reading the words. That is what good readers do.

Reading comprehension is something *everyone* can learn to do. Whether we call it improving our reading comprehension or memory of what we read or close reading or reading for information, with practice they will not even be aware that they are reading, but will instantly be absorbed in the movie they made in their mind as they turn the pages of the book. They may never have learned to read this way and suddenly find how enjoyable it is to have an entire movie playing out in their head as they turn the pages. This is why there are millions of people who enjoy reading—they are getting the experiential movie in their heads. Did you ever hear some people say they prefer reading the book to seeing the movie of the same title? Why? First, because they experience the book as a movie, imagining the scenes based on their own experiences. After all, that is what the filmmaker or screenwriter is doing. They have taken the same script they are reading in book form and converting it to images on the screen. When they read the book themselves they are the director, and they can determine the actors, actresses, and scenery, even putting themselves and people they know into the story and living it as if they are there. That is why it is so engrossing and engaging for some people to read and why they cannot put a book down until they are finished. Second, in a book they also experience the feelings and thoughts of the characters, while on a movie screen they can only infer the feelings and thoughts from the actors' facial expressions, tones of voice, or actions. They can relate to the characters, share their experience, and know that others go through many of the same emotions and thoughts that they have. They can also find solutions to their problems as they work through theirs.

Exercise: Practice Experiential Reading Comprehension with the Learners Own Reading Material:

For the purpose of the initial exercise, have the learner chose a fictional piece with descriptions of a person doing something. Take a paragraph or two and have them read it in the way described in the two sample passages above. Ask themselves what is happening in their movie and either describe it in their head or aloud. If they want a partner to help them, have the partner ask, "What is happening in your movie?" Describe the scenes phrase by phrase, or sentence by sentence. Kinesthetic learners will act out the action. If they are a combination of superlink learning styles, they will combine several senses. After reading the page, ask themselves questions to recall what they read, or have someone ask questions about the passage for them. If the learner or their partner cannot think of the questions to ask, the learner can just relate back everything they remember that happened in their movie, and then check their response against the text to verify how much they recalled.

Eliminating Blocks to Reading and Listening Comprehension

There are several blocks to reading and listening comprehension that hinder us as we read or listen. Many people struggle to read and go through life never learning how to eliminate these blocks. They are: being unable to associate new learning with the knowledge they already have; misunderstanding the terminology and vocabulary; and being unable to break words down into syllables to figure out the longer words. This next section will take each of these factors and show them how to eliminate these problems to help accelerate their learning.

Hooking Information into Our Prior Knowledge

When we are first faced with information, the brain perceives it either visually, auditorially, tactilely, or kinesthetically, and asks one question: Do I recognize this information?" It searches its database of memories and comes up with three possible answers:

1) Yes, I already know this information.
2) No, I do not know this information at all.
3) It is similar to something I know, but different in some ways.

If the brain already knows the information, it just reconfirms it; it does not have to put in any further effort to alter its knowledge base. For example, while shopping in the grocery store we see the cauliflower stand and recognize "cauliflower." We do not give it much thought because we already know it.

If the brain decides that it does not know the information at all, then it has more work to do, slowing down the process. It has to create a new memory connection for the information and learn more about what "it" is. In most cases, the brain will try to avoid this step and stay with the step above—linking it to something it already knows because it is easier. For example, they are in the grocery store and they see a vegetable whose shape, color, and name they never saw or heard of before. They have no idea of what it tastes like, how to prepare it, where it comes from, and what it is used for. They have a lot of work to do to find additional data about this vegetable. Chances are if they came across the word for that vegetable in a text, they may recall seeing it, but have no idea what it is, and could not easily comprehend that text. It would be a lot of easier if someone said to them, "This vegetable is like squash, tastes like squash, but differs in shape and color." Then it would be easier for them to hook it into their memory bank with data on squash.

If the brain finds that the information is similar but not exactly like what is in its memory, it will evaluate the ways it is similar and how it differs. It will then link the new information to that specific memory that is similar, making an association with what it knows. The brain cuts down its work of assimilating the new information because it says, "Oh, it is just like that other thing I already have in my memory. I only have to remember what makes it different." It is easier to learn information associated with what we already know because we only need to accommodate the differences. For example, we see green cauliflower in the store. We stop and think, "Oh, this is something new. It looks like cauliflower in shape but like broccoli in color." You read the sign and it says, "Broccoflower." You now alter your mental database to accommodate a new form of cauliflower that is green like broccoli, or a new form of broccoli that looks like cauliflower, depending upon how you look at it.

Thus, the first step in comprehension is to make associations between the new material and the old. When we are learning something new, we want to find a way to connect it to our prior knowledge. Think of it as a computer database in which certain programs already exist in the hard drive. If we try to open a file in a program not installed on the hard drive, the computer would not be able to recognize and read it. We would have to convert the format of the program into what is on the hard drive to be able to "comprehend" it.

Understanding New Terminology and Vocabulary

We need to use terminology or vocabulary to understand new data. We may encounter a new object, concept, or idea, but unless we can use terminology or vocabulary that we already have in our brain, we will not understand the meaning or function of the new data. It is like learning a word from another language. The word is only a collection of sounds and letters until we know its definition. Only then can we interpret the information and comprehend it.

If we are learning the material on our own and we come across an unfamiliar word, we need to first define it and then try to connect it to something similar in our memory. To define the new information, we may need to look in a reference source such as dictionary, glossary, or encyclopedia, either in a physical book form or online. If it is a term found while reading a physical book or eBook, then the first time the information appears we need to look back to previous pages where it will usually be defined. There, we can find written examples or graphic illustrations. In an eBook, we can click on a link and an elaboration or definition of the word appears. We can also ask someone what it means.

We need to take responsibility for finding the definition. Often, when we do not know a new term, we just skip over it for one reason or another. This is how we develop faulty reading comprehension: By not bothering to find out what each new bit of information means, we create a gap in our understanding. Suppose that information turns up again over and over in the material. Our comprehension continues to drop because further knowledge is dependent upon the terms we skipped. This could happen when we are reading, listening to a lecture, or in doing a procedure. If we do not take the time to understand the meaning of each term, we will fumble because we will not understand the material.

Hopefully, when we are learning from an instructor or from print material, audio-visual or digital material, or computers, the presentation will adequately ensure that new information is properly defined for us. However, there is no way to know what the learner already knows from his or her prior education. Thus, it is up to us as learners to ask for clarification when something is new or unfamiliar, and learn how to look up information in reference materials ourselves.

As we learn, we should keep track of any vocabulary or terminology we do not understand. If the learner is visual, tactile, or kinesthetic, write it down as a reminder to look up the definition at the first available opportunity. If the learner is auditory, they should stop and ask questions as soon as it is feasible. If Kinesthetic, they can use their superlink learning style to define the word in the following ways:

Kinesthetic Left-Brain: The learner will take a large paper and, while standing up, write the word and its definition in a list and relate it to an action to go with the meaning. Act out the word in a situation in which it would be used. If that is not possible, imagine themselves acting out an action situation that involves the word. Do a movement activity (walking, jogging in place, tossing a ball in the air) as they read through their list of words and their definitions.

Kinesthetic Right-Brain: The learner will take large paper and, while standing up, write the word in large size and in color with the definition arranged as a mind map with an action drawing in color accompanying the meaning. Act out the word in a situation that relates to the word. Imagine themselves acting out a situation that would involve the word, or make up an imaginative action story using the new word, other words they already know that sound similar, and the definition of the word. Do a physical activity, such as bouncing a ball, jogging in place, or pedaling on an exercise bike, etc., while reading back their word and the meanings.

They will find that it will be easier to learn the meanings of unfamiliar words and terms when they do so in their best superlink learning style.

Reading Words Syllable by Syllable

The techniques in this chapter can be used for several purposes. They can eliminate blocks to reading comprehension due to not knowing how to read all the sounds in English. They can also be applied to learning a different language. Finally, they can be used to learn symbols in various technical languages, such as computer languages, science, math, or any other fields that have specialized symbols.

One difficulty that prevents us from understanding the meanings of the words we read, either in English or in another language, is that we may not be able to say a word because we do not know what sounds the letters make. English is a complicated language because one letter may have many phonetic sounds. There are a surprising number of adults whom I have met, many with high school and even college degrees, who cannot properly read passages aloud that contain multisyllabic words or a higher-level vocabulary because they do not know phonics or how to read the more complicated phonetic letter patterns in those words. The same holds true for many high school and college students who struggle with reading text at those levels. Many of them find their comprehension suffers because they end up skipping over the "hard" words. In some languages, you only have to learn one sound for each letter, but, in English phonics, did you know that there are more than twenty-five ways to read and spell the letter *o*, depending upon which letters it is next to? For example, *o* can be pronounced and combined with different letters to give us: *hot, rope, go, toe, boat, book, boot, out, through, bought, dough, rough, could, cow, row, other, or, tore, door, soar, doll, troll, hole, goal, oil, and boy*, etc. If someone does not learn all the possible combinations for each vowel sound, it is easy to misread words. Thus, many people have reading problems both in English and in other languages because they have not learned all the letter-sound, phonics, or phonetic combinations. How did this happen? A startling number of students in upper grades and college, as well as adults, cannot convert the letters they see on the page into the correct sounds, because they never learned or mastered the phonics or letter-sound relationships or phonetic patterns. Often adults notice this problem for the first time only when they are given technical reading material, professional journals, or training materials to read at the workplace, or they take a test for their job, and they suddenly realize they do not have all the tools to tackle the task. They considered themselves readers, and often did not notice the problem because many popular books, magazines, and newspapers are written at a lower reading level. These adults may have previously figured out words only from their contexts. Sometimes they may have been accurate and at other times they may have been far from the right word due to guessing the actual word. As a result, they either read the wrong word and did not comprehend the reading material or they skipped the word and were left with a gap in their reading comprehension.

Some may use the letters they see, but when they do not know the correct sounds, their brain may do a word search and pops out with a word made of a mix of those letters, but which are not the actual word. If they do this, they generally are guess-reading the word and it is often not the accurate word. The results of these various strategies is that they either have read the wrong word and do not comprehend what they read accurately, or they have a gap in their knowledge because they skipped the word.

Some people can comprehend what they read when they know all the words, but when they cannot read the words correctly, it seems that they have a comprehension problem. In fact, they may not have a reading comprehension problem; they have a letter-sound relationship or phonics problem. Someone may try to help them by giving endless comprehension exercises to boost their abilities in that area, but their problem is a different one—they need to learn how to read the words before they can answer questions based on what they actually read—not what they guessed they read.

If the learner struggles with hard words, it may be because they do not know the correct pronunciation of some phonics patterns. If they do not have this difficulty, they can still apply the following section to learning the letter-sound relationships or phonics of English or any other language based on phonics patterns. If they have to learn a second language, they will accelerate their learning by using their best superlink learning style. To accelerate reading instruction, all the letter-sound relationships or phonics patterns should be taught in the first year, along with comprehension, vocabulary, and independent reading strategies. If, instead of just learning a few of the sounds in the first year of reading, students of all ages learned *all* the sounds in that first year, they would accelerate their reading abilities and comprehension as well as their speed.

Another factor that may have caused a problem with word reading is that many people did not grasp the sounds various letters made because the first time they learned it they were not taught it in their best learning style. Letter-sound relationships or phonics can be learned through one's best superlink learning style. Entire schools and school districts who initially had two-thirds of their students not meeting state standards in reading due to their lack of knowledge of all the phonics patterns discovered that when students were taught phonics in an accelerated way through each student's best superlink learning style, the district or school rose to two-thirds of the students meeting and exceeding state reading standards in eight months or less (less than one school year.) The result of those initial errors in accurately reading the words caused gaps in their reading comprehension; however, when their word-reading ability improved, their comprehension scores also rose. When there are word-reading gaps, it makes a big, gaping hole in the imaginary movie readers make in their minds. Although some may use strategies, such as using the first letter of a word combined with the context to figure out what word makes sense, this may result in not actually reading the correct word, causing comprehension errors. This shows up as a critical problem when: a) the number of words at which the reader is guessing using only the context becomes too large and they no longer are reading the same exact passage that is printed; b) when tested, they guess the wrong word and do not answer the question correctly. (This can happen not only on straight reading comprehension tests, but in any content area subjects such as science, social studies, or math); c) they become so used to "guess reading" that when they enter the job market, someone discovers they misread directions or instructions critical to getting their job done accurately. Has it ever occurred to anyone that the reason why two-thirds of the nation's students struggle with reading, according to the United States Department of Education statistics, is that many cannot even read the words? We may think it is due to reading comprehension problems alone, but it could be that their comprehension is fine; it is their knowledge of vocabulary or ability even to read the words using phonics patterns that are lacking.

Some people may graduate school and still not know all the letter-sound relationships or phonics patterns, either because it was not taught, or if it were taught, it was not taught in their best superlink learning style. Some people might have been taught these letters-sound relationships only partially or piecemeal but did not learn *all* the phonics patterns. What this means is that they may learn a few phonics patterns in a first grade reading class, a few more in a second grade reading class, and some more in third grade, and the rest in the upper grades of elementary school. Yet children are exposed or asked to read to all letter-sound relationships or phonics patterns in written material from the very beginning years of school, including first and second grade. They are given books to read in which all the letter-sound relationships or phonics patterns of English appear. At the earlier stages, they can only sound out a few patterns they learned. They may pick up several hundred easy words by sight. However, what happens when they get a new and unfamiliar word? As long as they have picture clues in young reader books in first and second grade, they can guess the meaning from context, but when the pictures become less and the number of new words increases dramatically, such as from third and fourth grade and higher, they have to guess too many words from the context to even make sense of what they are reading. Thus, the earlier they are taught all the letter-sound or phonics patterns of English (or any other language based on phonics), the fewer gaps they will have in their reading and the more they will read fluently, comprehending fully what they read. If instead of just teaching a few of the sounds in first grade or in the first year of reading, students of all ages, including adults, learned all the sounds in their first year of study, they would accelerate their reading abilities, fluency, and reading comprehension, as well as their speed. They will not be slowed down by rereading the sentence repeatedly to guess the context. They also will not be slowed down because they failed a test and had to retake the course as they did not know how to read all the words!

The key to learning the letter-sound or phonics relationships the first time around is to learn it in the learner' best superlink learning style. The following are techniques to use to learn the letter-sound or phonics patterns for the kinesthetic left-brain and right-brain superlink learning style and brain styles:

Kinesthetic Left-Brain Learners: The learner will write the letter in the air in large print with the arm muscles of their writing hand, or write the letter on the wall with a flashlight using all your arm muscles. The learner will stand up and write the letter in large size on a flip chart, chalkboard, or dry-erase white board. They will use large three-dimensional letter blocks and move them around to make words. They will draw the letters in chalk on the sidewalk about six feet tall, and walk along the letters, saying them as they go. They will learn any rules for pronouncing the letter. The learner can play step-by-step games to learn the patterns.

Kinesthetic Right-Brain Learner: The learner will write the letter in the air with the arm they use for writing, or write it on the ceiling with a flashlight. They will write the letter large while standing up at a flip chart and draw an action picture that starts with the letter. Use large three-dimensional letter blocks and have the learner move them around to make words. They will walk along the letter drawn on a sidewalk while saying it and seeing it. Make the letter with their body while saying it and seeing it. Do an action that starts with the letter and say and see the letter as they do the action. As they say the letter and words that start with it, throw a basketball into a net, bounce a ball, or do some activity with their body. Hang up the letters and words where they can see them, and read the letter and matching words while doing an activity or their favorite hobby, such as pedaling on an exercise bike, walking around the room, hitting a golf ball, jumping rope, or throwing a basketball, etc. Give themselves points each time they read the word and make a basket. Reward themselves for a certain number of points. The learner can play games to learn the patterns.

These are only some sample activities for each kinesthetic superlink learning style to learn to accurately read words and understand the phonics of the English language to read to college and adult level books. For anyone who feels they cannot accurately read words, especially larger, multi-syllable words and finds oneself skipping the "big words" which results in gaps in comprehension, the following resources can help, created for the different learning styles and brain styles. If the learner wants to boost their word reading level from where they are to college and adult level reading in an average of only 10 weeks, *Off the Wall Phonics*™ provides 10 levels (one per week) with 10 games in each level for a quick, fun way to master all the patterns and is proven to work. By working through 10 brief five-to-ten minute activities a day, and mastering each level per week, they will be able to read and decode larger multisyllable words at the college and adult level in 10 weeks. It is designed for kinesthetic and tactile learners who need to learn by moving and using their hands, but with its visuals and its auditory soundtrack it is also ideal for the visual and auditory learners. This is available from: www.offthewallphonics.com or www.readinginstruction.com. For more activities for each superlink learning style you can refer them to the following resources, such as my other books: *Solving Your Child's Reading Problems*; *Your Child Can Be a Great Reader*; *The Fine Line between ADHD and Kinesthetic Learning: 197 Kinesthetic Activities to Quickly Improve Reading, Memory, and Learning*; *Kinesthetic Vocabulary Activities; Tactile Vocabulary Activities;* plus two Internet Software programs to learn to read and improve in reading comprehension, memory, phonics, fluency, vocabulary, study skills, note taking, and test-taking skills, in one's superlinks learning style and brain style, *Keys to Reading Suc*cess™ and *Superlinks to Accelerated Learning*™ **(www.readinginstruction.com)**. Those interested in learning reading techniques using Superlinks learning styles and brain hemispheric preference styles can get more information from: National Reading Diagnostics Institute and Keys Learning in Naperville, Illinois.

When the student learns the letter-sound relationship or phonics patterns in English or another language through their correct superlinks learning style and brains style, learning is accelerated, easier, and more fun because they are working in their element.

What about Listening Comprehension?

The examples in this chapter describe comprehension tasks as related to reading, but listening comprehension involves the same skills. The same strategies for using our best learning style and brain style described in the above sections on comprehending what we read can be used to comprehend what we hear when listening to a speaker, either in person, through streaming audio or video on the web, in the movies, or on any digital audio or video device.

Pulling It All Together to Accelerate Progress in Improving Reading Comprehension

By involving the learner's superlink learning style and brain style in using the reading and teaching strategies in this chapter, they can gain a fuller understanding while improving their memory of everything they read and hear, empowering them to comprehend and master the subject they are studying at an accelerated rate.

CHAPTER 6: HOW TO LEARN TO IMPROVE AND INCREASE MEMORY USING THE LEARNER'S SUPERLINKS LEARNING STYLE AND BRAIN STYLE

Did you know that anyone could improve and increase their memory by using their superlink learning style and brain style? A good memory is not something that some people are born with and some lack. Memory *can* be developed by anyone. The only difference between someone with a good memory and someone with a poor one is training. This chapter provides a practical, quick, and easy-to-use guide of strategies and techniques to improving memory using one's superlink learning style and brain style to accelerate learning.

Training Memory

We have a tremendous amount of data stored in our brain that we can pull up at will. One reason we do not remember certain things is that we did not make an *effort* to remember them longer for an extended period of time. Consciously or unconsciously, we *chose* to remember those items we do remember. If we want to improve our memory, we can do so by training ourselves to remember what we want when we want.

When we talk of learning anything quickly, we want to learn the subject as well as recall it for more than just a moment. Sadly, when many instructors teach a subject, the students know it only until they are tested on it. Give them a surprise test a month or two later and all that hard work to learn the subject seems to have been for naught. How is it possible that we can spend six months to a year taking a course and forget what we learned years later? It is not that we do not have a good memory—we just do not have a *trained* memory. Accelerated learning involves training our memory using our superlink learning style and brain style.

Long-term and Short-term Memory

We have two memory systems: short-term and long-term memory.

Short-term memory holds something temporarily in our mind until we decide what to do with it. Consciously or unconsciously, we can either decide to store it in our long-term memory or dismiss it as something unimportant. Our short-term memory is a revolving door with new information entering continually. It can be compared to a computer screen memory. Information stays there as long as we are focusing on it and working with it. Then we must decide whether to save it in the hard drive—the computer's long-term memory—or let it be erased when we turn the computer off.

Long-term memory permanently holds something in our memory. There are many things we learned in childhood that were placed in our long-term memory that we have not forgotten: walking; riding a bicycle, speaking our language; writing the alphabet, or childhood songs and nursery rhymes; among other things. These memories become a part of our database from which we can draw at any time.

Keys to Improving Memory

The basics of having a good memory are simple and can be learned by people of any age, including young children. Anyone *can* improve their memory.

Step 1) Having a purpose or goal for remembering what is being learned.

Step 2) Consciously deciding to put what is learned into long-term memory.
Step 3) Use the learner's superlink learning style and brain style to store what has been learned into long-term memory.
Step 4) Keeping one's memory active by retrieving it and using it.

Step 1: Having a Purpose or Goal for Remembering what is Being Learned

We are bombarded with millions of bits of information daily. With the opening of the Internet, the information superhighway, we have access to a huge amount of information circulating in the world on a daily basis. If we were to recall every single sensory impression and bit of information we receive we would be so overwhelmed we would not be able to focus on the range of activities that were more important to our lives. Life is too short to learn everything about everything; we must make a conscious choice about what we want to remember. This process involves deciding why we need to learn something. When we want to learn something, we must also decide why it is important for us to learn it. If we keep that goal in mind, we will put our brain on notice that this is material we *want* to remember.

Why did we remember our name as a child? When we figured out that people kept asking us our name, we decided that next time they asked we had better know it or they may think there is something wrong with us. Why did we learn those twenty-six meaningless sounds called the "alphabet" when we were just a toddler? We had no idea what they stood for or what words they went with, but we learned how to repeat these twenty-six sounds that might well have been nonsense to us. Why did we learn it? Maybe we figured out that our parents would show us off to their friends by having us repeat the alphabet and would give us that big smile and hug that we loved. Or maybe we surmised that our relatives would give us a monetary award for being such a "good and smart" child for saying our "ABCs." We had a purpose for learning that information at age two, three, or four, which had nothing to do with getting a high school diploma. We could have just as easily been taught the ABCs in a foreign language, or the periodic table of the elements, or the names of all the bones of the body. We learned what we did because someone valued it, rewarded us for knowing it with either verbal or nonverbal gestures or material gifts, and this made us feel good.

The same principle holds true today when it comes to learning. We really wanted to learn how to drive so we mastered the physical act of driving along with the driver's manual with all its facts, figures, and state laws. The same people who cannot pass a social studies test can pass a written driving examination on technical information and legal terms. Why? They wanted to remember the driver's education manual because it meant if they could learn how to drive they could have wheels. It is the same brain that is reading that driver's education manual that is reading other textbooks. Is there a selective gene in our body that discriminates between learning a driver's education manual and a political science course? Not at all. It is our intention and desire to learn something that determines what we will remember and what we will forget.

Some possible reasons, purposes, or goals for learning are: to get a job or advance in our career; to improve our skills; to raise our salary; to get a promotion; to become certified in a field; to pass a test; to keep up with new knowledge; to help others; for enjoyment, personal growth or curiosity; or for many other reasons.

EXERCISE: Take the subject the learner chose to study as they worked through this book and write a sentence or two stating why they want to learn more about this subject.

Step 2: Consciously Deciding to Put What Is Learned into Long-Term Memory

We must program our minds to send information into our long-term memory if we wish to retain it. Otherwise, we will get the information, comprehend it, but it will be erased shortly afterwards. If we want to recall it for the long haul, we have to establish the reason for wanting to put it into long-term memory and the length of time we want it to stay in memory. Many people find they lack study skills and test-taking skills because they cannot remember what they read, hear, or study long enough to pass a test. That is because they do not program themselves to recall everything they learn for the entire duration of the course of study.

Here are some things to think about as the learner is trying to commit what they want learn to long-term memory:

1) If they learn it the first time they read or hear it they won't have to go over the material again and again, wasting precious time.

2) They can use what they learn to work towards their job promotion, advancement, or passing a test, certification exam, or course faster.

3) They will have more free time to do other things.

4) They will be able to use the information right away.

Have them decide that they want to commit what they learn to their long-term memory, the length of time they want to retain it, and why it is important for them to learn it.

EXERCISE: Using the subject they selected to learn as they work through this book, write their reasons for putting what they learn about the subject into long-term memory.

Step 3: Use the Learner's Superlink Learning Style and Brain Style to Store What They Learn into Long-Term Memory

This is the key to the entire process. I developed this technique as an extension of the application of superlinks learning styles and brain styles. It works so incredibly quickly that everyone who has used it is amazed at how sharp his or her memory becomes.

The secret is: The key to improving one's memory and remembering what has been learned is to store it according to their best superlink learning style and brain style.

If the learner is a kinesthetic learner, they remember best what they did and how their body moved.

Did the learner remember their experiential reading comprehension? As they read or listened, they converted the information into an experience in their mind that matched their superlink learning style and brain style.

Kinesthetic people would ***act out*** the actions and events of the movie in their minds.

By experiencing what was read or heard using their superlink learning style and brain style, they are causing their mind to think an event is really happening to them. They have involved themselves into a true virtual reality experience that is taking place inside their mind through their best sense, supported by the other senses.

Books or lectures are real events that have been converted into words for the benefit of those who were not there. Writing is like creating a cyberworld in which reality is encoded into words, and reading decodes or converts it back into experiences and events. Reading is like cracking a code so we can recreate the writer or speaker's experience in our minds. The more vividly we do this and the more we involve ourselves in the action, the more we will experience being there and the more thoroughly we will remember it.

Review the chapter on reading comprehension with the learner in which they learned how to use experiential comprehension to match their superlink learning style and brain style. This method will increase their memory of what they read. They can review the sample reading passage or select one of their own. Another optional passage the learner can use for reading comprehension and memory practice is given below in Exercise 1. As they read, make a commitment to put this information into long-term memory. Attempt to remember *all* the details of this passage, including names, dates, and other factual information. Read it according to their superlink learning style and brain style. Convert it into a movie in their mind, either seeing it, hearing it, feeling it, or doing the actions involved. Make associations for words, numbers, and dates, finding similar words or images already in their mind.

After reading the passage, cover it up and discover how much of it they remember now that they have experienced it as an actual event. If they imagined the story in their best superlink learning style and brain style, they should have found that they can answer every question and recall every detail after converting it into a movie scene based on their preferred sense. If he or she missed any questions or details, analyze why. Most likely they did not make a strong enough experience in their mind or they skipped over part of the text without imagining it. It is always fascinating to find that any text that someone did not imagine as a movie in their best superlink learning style is gone from his or her memory when he or she tries to answer the questions, while the material that the person *did* imagine in his or her superlink style pops out as if he or she really experienced the event.

The learner can do this kind of reading with everything they read, fiction or nonfiction, including informational texts. They can try this with reading the daily news whether printed in a newspaper or Internet news site, magazine or ezine articles, trade journals, memos, newsletters, interoffice communications, text messages, E-mail, faxes, flogs, social media sites, or websites. The same technique can work with a novel as well as with scientific material, technical reading, history, the social sciences, health, medical books, training materials for any field, textbooks on any subjects, or anything else they can think of. They can also use it for listening comprehension when listening to lectures. Auditory left-brain people can mentally record material directly in their minds, while those with other superlinks learning styles and brain styles can take dictation so they can convert the material into an experiential event later at their own pace in their own quickest way of learning.

Anyone can train themselves to read or listen to any material and put it into long-term memory. What does it take? All the learner has to do is be mentally present as they read. The moment they just look at the words without converting them, they have actually stopped reading. Reading only takes place when the words become images or experiences in their mind. Unless they are an auditory left-brain person who gets meaning directly from words, without converting them into corresponding experiences in their superlink learning style and brain style, just reading (for other learning styles) "word, word, word, word" continually without images is not only NOT READING, it is a boring, useless task that does not help them. Begin to monitor their reading by making sure they are converting every word they read into experiences. Remember, the moment they stop making movie scenes in their superlink learning style and brain style, they have stopped reading. They have begun to daydream or mentally wander. Every word they may have looked at or even said aloud while their mind wandered is gone from their memory because they were not really mentally present. They will then need to return to the last set of words that they imaged and reread that section using the virtual reality experiential reading comprehension technique or it may be lost.

If they are reading to learn, they will soon realize that when they do not image the text as they read, they are wasting precious time. Not only do they *not* comprehend the information, they will not be sending it into long-term memory. That is why they may have had to read the same material over and over in the past. But if they are in a hurry and want to learn anything quickly, they need to read it correctly the first time around. They will find that with a little practice they can have total recall and memory of everything they read. Just be attentive, do the conversion process in their best learning style and brain style, and with hardly any effort, the whole passage will come back to them hours, days, or even weeks later because they transformed it into an experience that happened to them. This method of reading comprehension and memory that I developed and tested with people of all ages is a powerful tool they will have to speed up their reading and learning.

As they answered the reading comprehension questions for the sample passage, they may have noticed that as certain key words in the questions came up, an image or memory arose in their mind. If they are not auditory and they tried to remember the words, they may have drawn a blank. But if they instead said to themselves, "What did I experience in my movie?" while they were in a relaxed mental state, the movie would have rerun in their head and the answer would have appeared. They were using both their right and left hemisphere of the brain in this process. The image appears in the side of the brain that can picture it (usually the right side of the brain), and the word for it is recalled from their speech and language centers in the brain (usually the left side of the brain, although some people have some language in the right side of the brain). Thus, they have engaged their whole brain in this process. This kind of reading comprehension and memory is a great exercise for developing their whole brain. They are making more connections between the two halves of the brain and developing their thinking and memory powers as well.

Memory Improvement Exercise 1: The learner can use this sample passage to further practice the experiential virtual reality reading comprehension and memory technique in their Superlinks learning style and brain style, or, if they grasp how it works, they can move on to Exercise 2 to practice it with an actual subject they want to read or study.

Next, the instructor will model for the learner how you can work together through the following sample practice reading comprehension and memory passage, "Dave," making a commitment that the learner will want to put this information into long-term memory. The task is to attempt to remember *all* the details of this passage, including names, dates, and other factual details. He or she will read it according to their superlink learning style and brain style. Both sides of their brain will be involved, the right and left side, for this exercise to show them how they can remember both the big picture and graphic images (right-brain functions) as well as every detail and the words for the experience (left-brain functions). Thus, they will engage both sides of the brain in the process of reading the sample passage called "Dave." Although the entire passage appears below, do not read it yet, but skip down to "Instructions for Reading the Sample Practice Reading Comprehension and Memory Passage: 'Dave'" and let it guide the learner to read the sample passage in small chunks as directed.

Sample Practice Reading Comprehension and Memory Passage: "Dave"

Dave looked at his watch as he rushed out of his apartment. It was Monday morning and he was late again. As he ran down the steps of his apartment building, heading towards his red sports car, he felt the humid air pressing in on him. It was going to be another hot summer day in June. Dave opened his car door, tossed his brown attaché case onto the passenger seat, and slid into the driver's side. This was the only thing he looked forward to every morning, driving his new car along the freeway to his office. He looked forward to next week when he would begin a two-week vacation. As he drove towards Interstate 72, his mind raced along thinking about his holiday. "Aruba sounds good with its dry air, its seventy-degree weather, and its cool ocean breezes—a change from this stifling humidity," he thought to himself. A short ring from his cell phone startled him out of his daydream.

Instructions for Reading the Sample Passage "Dave": Now, the instructor and the learner will read through this passage together, using the kinesthetic superlink learning style and brain style to convert this into an experience that he or she will save in their long-term memory. As they read, kinesthetic people will be experiencing ***doing*** the actions of what is happening. Ready to roll the scene?

The learner can make it a movie, a theater production, or a real-life event happening to them. Ready? Lights, camera, action:

The passage first says: "Dave looked at his watch as he rushed out of his apartment." Make an image in his or her mind of Dave. Think of someone named Dave that he or she knows, either a personal relationship or an actor, athlete, or someone famous, so they can remember his name. Or, he or she can become Dave for this movie, and look at their watch. Describe their watch in their Superlinks learning style (kinesthetic learners may experience themselves doing an exercise along with the moving of the secondhand of the watch). Next, experience themselves rushing out of their apartment. Based on their superlink learning style they will imagine: What action is going on in the apartment?

Read the next phrase: "It was Monday morning...." Think, "How will he or she remember Monday morning? What images come to them when they think of Monday? How would they portray Monday on a movie screen to let the audience know that it is Monday?" Kinesthetic learners may feel their car speed up and slow down in the stop and go traffic as they drive to work during Monday morning rush-hour traffic. The key is to think of an association that will help them remember the word "Monday."

Now read the next phrase: "...and he was late again." See, hear, feel, or experience what it is like to be late again. What is going on inside their mind when they are late? Are their muscles tightening up in preparation for fighting the good fight in rush-hour traffic?

Continue with the next phrase: "As he ran down the steps of his apartment building...." The learner will imagine (see, hear, feel, or experience) themselves running down the steps of an apartment building. What is the apartment building like? If kinesthetic, what actions can he or she do in the apartment building? What is happening on their movie screen, theater production, or real-life experience?

Next, read "...heading towards his red sports car..." Get a red sports car imaged in their mind. Think, "What does it look like? How does it sound? What does it feel like to own one and how does it feel to be in it? What do their muscles experience as they drive it?"

"...he felt the humid air pressing in on him." Think, "What does it look like when it is humid out? What does it sound like to have humid air pressing in on them? What does it feel like? What do their muscles do when they feel humidity?"

"It was going to be another hot summer day in June." Think, "How would he or she portray to an audience a hot summer day in June? Would they show children in bathing suits running through lawn sprinklers to cool down? What comes to their mind when they think of June? Do they think of someone's birthday? Are they at a June wedding? Whatever meaningful association they have for June use it. Remember, they want to hook this month into their prior knowledge, or whatever else is already in their head related to June. But don't use the instructor's examples—they must make up their own or it will not mean anything to them!

"Dave opened his car door..." Does the learner have this image of themselves opening a car door? They will be either seeing it, hearing it, feeling it, or doing it.

"...tossed his brown attaché case onto the passenger seat..." Image in his or her mind a brown attaché case either that they own, or one that they saw. Note that they are tossing it onto the passenger seat. Image in his or her mind the passenger seat in their own car or someone's car they know.

"...and slid into the driver's side." The learner will do this now. Slide into the driver's seat of their car. Kinesthetic Learners will imagine themselves doing it.

"This was the only thing he looked forward to every morning, driving his new car along the freeway to his office." What would someone look like with this attitude? Does the learner see him smiling as he gets in? Kinesthetic learners will ask, "Do you experience racing that car along the highway?"

"He looked forward to next week when he would begin a two-week vacation." Visualize themselves packing their suitcases.

Now, focus on remembering the number "two"—what images come to his or her mind for "two?" Can they feel themselves *jump* off a diving board with their *two* feet? The learner needs to find an association for the number two that is meaningful to them and experience it in their learning style.

"As he drove towards Interstate 72..." Another number—72. First the learner will experience themselves driving towards the interstate. He or she will experience an interstate they know in their own state. Now, work on the number 72. The learner can make any number of associations—what happened to them or what happened in the world in 1972? Or take it as 7 and 2. What can he or she associate with 7 and what do they think of for number 2? Is there something that costs 72 dollars, someone who is 72 years old, some football player who wears number 72? Make the association happen on the interstate so they can connect these two together.

"...his mind raced along thinking about his holiday." Imagine themselves thinking about their own holiday as they drive along. Personalize it so he or she will remember it.

"Aruba sounds good with its dry air..." Now work on the name, Aruba." What images come to mind for the learner? Do they see or hear an ad for Aruba on television? Feel what it would be like to go to Aruba. What would someone do in Aruba? If they have no images, then take the word itself and think of something they already know that sounds like it or take the word apart and find smaller words that sound like those parts. For example, a-rub-a can be like a ruby—see a red ruby. Or take the spelling instead of the sound—rub—a rub down on your back as you lay out on the beach. Or connect "arid" or dry to Aruba and say "arid Aruba" and experience arid, dry air. What does he or she experience themselves doing in the arid, dry air?

"... it's seventy degree weather..." Another number—70 degrees. The learner can connect it with their interstate 72 image and subtract 2 to get 70, or they can think of its own association. Some examples that others have used are: some address with 70, someone who is 70, something that happened in 1970, etc. Experience that 70-degree weather.

"'... and its cool ocean breezes—a change from this stifling humidity,' he thought to himself." Now do something in cool ocean breezes. Is he or she surfing, swimming, sun bathing? Experience the stifling humidity. Do they hear themselves complaining about the humidity? Do they feel sticky? Do they experience themselves jumping in a cold shower to wash off that humidity? Image themselves thinking these thoughts to themselves.

"A short ring from his cell phone startled him out of his daydream." The learner will be in their car, experiencing themselves grabbing it and putting it up to their ear. Experience themselves snap back to reality from their daydream.

Now, do a practice reading comprehension and memory test to see how much the learner remembers of the story having made it in an experience that happened to them in their mind. The following questions will be answered, *without* looking back at the story. The answers are at the end of this section of this chapter, but no peeking or the point of this practice reading comprehension and memory exercise will be lost!

1. Name who this story is about.
2. In what kind of place does he live?
3. What time of day does the story begin?
4. What is the weather like outdoors?
5. What month of the year is it?
6. Where is he going that morning?
7. Is he on time?
8. What kind of car does he own and what color is it?
9. What route will he take?
10. What is his favorite activity each morning?
11. Where is he thinking about going on vacation?
12. When is he going on his vacation?
13. What is the weather like in the place he is going for his vacation?
14. What is the temperature like in the place he is going for his vacation?
15. What happens to him as he drives to work?

If the learner imaged the story in their best superlink learning style and brain style as they were guided through the reading, they should have found, as does everyone else who has successfully used this technique, that they were able to answer every question for which they made a strong image in their mind. If they missed any questions, analyze why. Most likely they missed a question because they did not make a strong enough image in their mind or they skipped it without imagining it. It is always fascinating to see that the movie scenes that people do not make are gone from their memory when they try to answer the questions, while the movie scenes they did make pop out as if they really experienced the event for themselves!

If the learner will convert each detail of what they read and hear into this experiential event or movie in their mind, they will be able to put into long-term memory everything they wish. He or she can do this kind of reading with everything they read, fiction or nonfiction. He or she can do this with the physical or digital texts, such as the daily newspaper, magazine articles, trade journals, memos, bulletins, interoffice communications, blogs, e-mail, faxes, website or social media sites. The same technique can work with a novel as well as with science material, technical reading, history, social sciences, health, textbooks in any content area subjects, medical books, training manuals for any field, and anything else they can think of.

The next question the learner may ask is, "Doesn't it take a long time to read this way?" The reply is, "no, it is actually quicker." It only seemed longer because they are just learning the technique and the instructor had to "talk" them though this initial practice reading comprehension and memory exercise to train him or her to read or listen in this way. The instructor was guiding the learner with a series of questions advising them on what to think about as they read, but the learner will take over from here and begin to ask themselves the questions as they read: "What am I seeing (hearing, feeling, or doing) now in my experience or movie?" When the learner thinks this, it takes only a few seconds. As they practice this technique for several weeks, they will not need to ask the question anymore--they will automatically begin to see, hear, feel or experience the action as they read. After a few weeks or months, he or she will find that the moment they read the words, the image appears. Soon, reading will be like a continual movie playing in their head in which they are not even conscious of the words at all. They will actually read faster because they will be immediately experiencing the images and they will move along continually without stopping at phrases anymore. Best of all, the learner will have increased and improved their memory to read and recall everything they choose!

Memory Improvement Exercise 2:

Find something to read on the subject the learner has chosen to learn. Take two or three paragraphs and practice reading them as shown in the example readings in this chapter. After each phrase, he or she will ask themselves what are they doing with their hands (if learner is a tactile learner), or doing with their large motor muscles or experiencing (if learner is a kinesthetic learner). Read the entire passage in that way. Then put the book down and see how many details he or she can recall, focusing on names, dates, places, and small facts. Practice reading this way with all reading material from now on until the learner finds they can make the movie images automatically, the moment they scan the words.

Answers to questions on the Sample Practice Reading Comprehension and Memory Passage: "Dave":

1) Dave; 2) an apartment or apartment building; 3) morning; 4) humid, or hot and humid; 5) June; 6) to work; 7) no, he is late; 8) red sports car; 9) Interstate 72 or the freeway; 10) driving his car on the freeway (or to work); 11) Aruba; 12) next week; 13) dry air, cool ocean breezes, or seventy-degree weather; 14) seventy degrees; 15) a phone call.

Step 4) Keeping that Memory Active by Retrieving It and Using It

The next step is to make sure the information the learner reads stays in their mind, as an active file, readily accessible at their fingertips, by deciding how often they need to use the information they learned and for what purposes. Have the learner think of it as having material immediately accessible on their computer's hard disk as opposed to putting it on flash sticks or thumb drives and filing them somewhere deep in their closet.

There may be certain types of information that are only needed for a one-time purpose. The learner may need to pass a test or exam and never need that information again. Suppose he or she took an art history course that was required for their fine arts degree. They do not want to go into art history, but they do want to be an artist. The learner needs the information to pass the test for their degree, but they do not want to load their mind with dates of famous paintings. Thus, the learner consciously decides to retain that data only so long as they need it to pass the examination and then let it go. They no longer want to work at keeping that memory active. Thus, they do not devote any more attention on it, and they do not use it or retrieve it anymore. Therefore, it is buried by newer, more relevant data that the learner needs to learn.

Step four in training the learner's memory involves making a conscious choice about which long-term memories they wish to keep in an active file and which ones he or she will allow to be buried in an inactive state. To keep a file active we need to use it and retrieve it periodically. They may not use the dates of the paintings ever again in their life so they let them go, but if he or she worked as a tour guide in an art museum, they would use that information again and again. It would become a part of them, and they could instantly bring it from memory, whenever they needed it. If the learner took a computer course and needed to use what they learned on their jobs every day, they would not want to forget the information after the final examination. By using the information daily, the learner will strengthen the neural network or the interconnections that enable them to perform those functions. Retrieval becomes quicker and more automatic, for when they repeatedly use the information they made a conscious effort to learn; it becomes part of their long-term memory.

Step four requires the learner to: decide how long he or she wants to keep what they learned as an active long-term memory and when and how often they will need to use what they learned and to make a plan for retrieving and using it regularly. If the learner decides they need to use it for the one year in which they will be working at a particular job, then they need to spend time practicing using it, doing something with it, or retrieving it daily, weekly, or several times a week so it is fresh in their mind. Have the learner put it on their "to-do" list. If they are kinesthetic, do something with it. This will keep the memory active. The more they use it, the more automatic retrieving this memory will become.

Exercise: Using the subject the learner is learning as an example to practice the techniques in this book, decide how long they want to retain the information as an active long-term memory; when and how often they will need to use what they learned; and their personal plan for retrieving and using the material regularly.

What about Memorization?

Another kind of memory task is pure memorization, which involves recalling lists of facts and data. If the learner finds they have to memorize information just to pass a test or exam, then they can also use their superlink learning style and brain style to accomplish this task quickly.

I have developed eight different memorization techniques, one for each of the eight superlinks learning styles and brain styles. Try it with a list of data the learner needs to remember. Instruct them to practice the technique until it becomes automatic.

Take the data the learner is trying to learn and make associations with something they already know. It can be a word that sounds like or is spelled like the word they need to remember. It may be a person or thing that comes to their mind when they think of that word. The learner needs to make up a movie or story in their mind connecting the new word on the list with the old word. The story should be vivid, humorous, imaginative, or far-out—something that will catch their attention and stay in their mind. People having each of the various superlinks learning styles and brain styles will need to enact their associations into a story in a different way based on their superlink style.

The main difference between the left-brain and right-brain techniques is that left-brain people will need to remember the list in order. The right-brain people can make the associations without going in order unless this is required for a test or task; then the right-brain people can use the left-brain technique combined with their learning style.

Memorizing Data: Suppose the learner needs to recall the following list of words: cat, house, moon, apple, football. Here is how people with each of the different preferred superlinks brain and learning styles can do it:

Right-brain: Remember the associations without putting them in order.

Left-brain: Remember them in linear order. Here is one way to do it: Instruct the learner to take their hands and lay them palms down in front of them. Using their left hand first, count on their fingers, beginning with the pinkie, as follows: pinkie finger is one, ring finger is two, middle finger is three, pointer or index finger is four, and thumb is five. Now he or she will imagine that they are attaching each of the five words to each of their five fingers, in order, beginning with the word *cat*. You will

do it according to one of the following superlinks learning style techniques below:
Kinesthetic Technique: The Kinesthetic learner will need to act out the words: 1) They are a cat and are crawling around on the floor. Take hold of the owner's pinkie finger and pull him or her playfully to romp on the floor. 2. The learner is building a house and in their exercise room they hang ropes with large rings from which to swing. Experience themselves swinging from the rings that are shaped like the ring on their ring finger. 3. The learner is doing a handstand on the moon, balancing on their middle finger. 4. The learner is twirling an apple on their pointer finger and tossing it up and down in the air. 5. The learner catches a football with their thumb and then runs to the goal line to make a touchdown. Now, when he or she flicks each of their five fingers what else are they doing? Do they remember all the words?

Mnemonics as a Memory Device for Each Superlink Learning Style and Brain Style

Try another memory improvement technique with the learner, mnemonics, by using the first letter of each word to make either a new word or a sentence using words that begin with the same first letters as the words in the list. The left-brain people will put the letters in order, while the right-brain people can mix up the order to create other sentences or words.
The **kinesthetic people** will *stand up and write* the words in large print at a chalk board or white board, or will use big blocks or cut out shapes with the letters on them and move them around. Or they will experience themselves doing an action with the words in their minds.

For example, to remember the five words: *cat*, *house*, *moon*, *apple*, and *football*, here are a left-brain and a right-brain memory improvement technique:
Left-brain people can put the words in order to make the nonsense word: *chmaf*: *c* for *cat*; *h* for *house*; *m* for *moon*; *a* for *apple*; and *f* for *football*. Or they can make a sentence from the first letter of each word: *C*an *h*e *m*ake *a f*ire? Added to that can be the actual words as part of the story. Can he make a fire? Have the moon shining over the house, as the cat sitting, on a football, chews an apple by the fire.
Right-brain people can mix-up the order in any way. Since the right side sees all the letters of a word simultaneously and does not put things in sequential order, it can remember them as effectively in any order it likes. For example: "cham(p)." Replace *f* with *p* and associate the *f* with the word *football:* He was the champ in football.

Another technique is to make a sentence with the first letters of each word arranged in any order: *M*y *f*riend *h*as *a c*at. You can then add the relevant words to this sentence to make a story: While you were sitting in your house, under a full moon, your friend came over with the cat, which was playing with a football and an apple.

The key to improve and increase memory is to make associations that are meaningful to the learner, that are out of the ordinary, and that tie the new words to the old words in some way.

Improving Memory by Creating a Story

Another technique is to connect all the words to make a unified story in which the learner plays an active part. He or she will do one or a combination of the following based on their superlink learning style and brain style: see the story, hear the story, feel the story, or act out the story in their mind. The following is an example: "You and your cat were taken from the house and sent up to the moon. You had apples to eat on the way. When you got to the moon you played football together and it was fun because you could bounce really high."

Improve Memory of Vocabulary Words in English or Other Languages:

Learning any field often requires understanding new terminology and vocabulary, so this section will be useful to improve memory in many situations. This technique can be used to learn and improve memory of the meaning of new words, either English or other languages. Remember, the visual learners will make a visual image; the auditory learners will hear and say the words of the association; the tactile learners will feel it; and the kinesthetic learners will do some action with the words.

English Vocabulary Words:

abase: to lower, humiliate
abashed: embarrassed, ashamed

Step 1: Take the word and find another word that looks or sounds like it and is already in the learner's memory bank: Example: abase: sounds like *base*, something that is on the ground.

Step 2: Make up a story connecting the word the learner already knows with the meaning of the new word: for example, "I was so humiliated I wanted to sink into the *base* or the ground."

Step 3: Connect the story with the learner's superlink learning style and brain style. Kinesthetic learners will be playing a basketball game and when they lose, they are humiliated and will fall down on the base, or floor.

When he or she sees or hears the word *abase* in the story they created, the word will replayed like a movie in their head and the concept of humiliation and lowering will come up as a movie scene, giving them its meaning.

Let's try the next word: abashed: ashamed. The word *abashed* sounds and looks like *bashed.* When you bashed into the wall because you weren't looking, you were ashamed. See it, hear it, feel it, or do it based on the learner's superlink learning style and brain style, and the word is theirs.

Words in other languages: The same principle can be used for learning how to learn and improve the learner's memory and vocabulary for words in different languages. For example: Here are steps if he or she wants to remember the French word *maison,* which means "house."

Step 1: Think of a word that sounds like, looks like, or is similar to *maison*, or the parts of the word: May's son; my son; maize or corn; May sun.

Step 2: The learner will make up a story connecting the association with the meaning of the word. Let's take "May sun." Link the hot May sun in the sky and their house. The learner might come up with a sentence such as, "The May sunshine was beating down on my house."

Step 3: The learner will connect the story with their superlink learning style. Kinesthetic learners will act it out.

Let us try an example with a Spanish word *blanco*, which means "white" Connect *blanco* to a blank sheet of paper that is white. Now the learner has *blanco* as "white."

A Trained Memory Accelerates Learning

By improving their memory the learner can learn something correctly the first time and cut down the wasted study time rereading and restudying the same material. They can accelerate their learning by training their memory using their superlink learning style and brain style.

CHAPTER 7: HOW TO LEARN TO IMPROVE NOTE TAKING, STUDY SKILLS, AND TEST TAKING SKILLS THROUGH THE LEARNER'S SUPERLINKS LEARNING STYLE AND BRAIN STYLE

If this were a perfect world, many people would do away with tests and studying. The word *test* can instill fear in even the most fearless of people. Because people have experienced many painful repercussions from failing a test, taking these has become a dreaded task for many. The only people who seem actually to enjoy tests are the ones who consistently do well in them and feel a sense of achievement and accomplishment.

Let us analyze what a test is. A child learns how to walk and "tests" his or her ability by taking a few steps. We learn a golf swing, and "test" our ability by practicing. A test is a checkpoint of measuring our performance or knowledge. We do this all the time in everyday life. It is not meant to be a system of penalizing us, but a way to gauge or measure what we have mastered and what knowledge or skills we have not yet mastered and may need to relearn or review.

If we are learning something on our own, we should build in checkpoints along the way to insure that we have mastered each section. Breaking a large amount of material into smaller bits can help manage the subject better. There are three study aids that can help us manage the subject we are learning. They are note taking, study skills, and test-taking skills.

There are two applications for these skills. We traditionally associate note taking, study skills, and test-taking skills with learning from books in traditional classroom settings, seminars, and workshops. This chapter will help the student learn better in those situations. The second application is for performance tasks such as learning a skill, job, hobby, sport, dance, craft, or musical instrument, or training to use a computer or other forms of technology. While there may not be any tests we need to prepare for, note-taking, study skills, and test-taking skills can still be useful checkpoints. We may wish to take notes as we learn a performance task, review those notes when we do not have access to our teacher or trainer, and test ourselves by measuring our performance. Thus, as you instruct the learner in this chapter they can apply the information to course work or self-study, textbook or lecture-based courses, and performance tasks.

Note taking is a way to record what we are learning to shorten our review time. It provides us with a study guide so we do not have to reread material or listen to the lecture again.

Study skills are the techniques we use to make sure we improve our memory so we can understand and remember the material we are learning.

Test-taking skills are strategies to prepare us for taking a test.

In this chapter the learner will learn how to use their superlink learning style and brain style for note taking, study, and test-taking skills.

Improving Note-taking Skills

In the previous chapter, we discovered how to improve our memory to put what we have learned into long-term memory. We also learned the importance of repeatedly retrieving and using the information to keep it easily accessible. Note taking is one aid to help us in doing this.

We take notes to serve as a simple study sheet to review what we have already learned. The notes trigger our memory to keep what we learned fresh in our mind. It saves us from flipping through numerous pages of a book or hours of audio to trigger our memories. Instead of going through a fifty-page chapter, we can look through several pages of notes to remind us of what we learned.

When taking notes, we do not want to write every word we read and hear. That would be like taking dictation. Note taking is *not* taking dictation; rather, it is a writing key phrases to trigger our memory later on for what is already remembered in our head. Note taking goes hand in hand with experiential reading comprehension and memory techniques described earlier in this book; it is not supposed to take their place.

If the learner reads in the experiential reading comprehension mode that matches their superlink learning style and brain style and then uses the memory techniques that they learned in the last chapter, they already have the material in memory. Note taking allows the learner to jot down some key points to organize what they remember in smaller units. In this way, when he or she reviews or studies, they can group together their memories of one unit or section of a subject and go over those memories together. They can think of it as a way to organize the data in their computer into files or records. It is hard to manage a one-thousand page document, so the learner will break it up into smaller chapters and put them into separate files or folders. Note taking helps us to do that. Then, when we look at the key words we wrote, it brings back our memory of all the material in that unit. There are note-taking skills to match each superlink learning style and brain style. In this chapter the learner will find out how to take notes to match their superlink learning style and brain style.

Key Words Shorten the Note-taking Process

To accelerate learning, we want to shorten the amount of time and notes we will write and limit them to key words. A key word triggers our memory of longer sentences. We will be writing only key words in our notes and eliminating nonessential words such as articles like "the," "a," "these," "those," "that," "which," etc. We will only use adjectives if they are keys to understanding the nouns they modify. When longer words are repeated, we may make an abbreviation for them. If we will be repeating the same name of a person or place over, we may want to write it out the first time, and alongside it write the initials for it to use throughout the rest of our notes. For numbers we can write the numerical form. For "is" and "are" we may use a dash (-) or equal sign (=). For "and" we may use the plus sign (+) or ampersand sign (&). The learner can devise their own shortcuts for taking notes. Here are examples of converting a sentence into key words:

George Washington was the first president of the United States.

G.Washington-1st pres. of U.S.
George Washington—1st U.S. president.
Washington—1st U.S. pres.

Two Classifications of Note Taking—Left-Brain and Right-Brain

Since left-brain people learners to work in a linear, sequential way while right-brain learners prefer to see all the material at once, simultaneously, we have two basic techniques for taking notes. These methods are adapted further, based on the learning styles of visual, auditory, tactile, and kinesthetic learners, which will give you eight different techniques. First, we will look at the differences between the left-brain and right-brain note-taking techniques.

Left-brain Note Taking Technique

Left-brain note-taking needs to be in a linear and sequential order. The outline format, listing points in numerical, alphabetical, or chronological order, fits the natural way that left-brain learners think. There are two basic techniques that use linear order that are helpful for left-brain people.

Technique 1: Left-brain Outlining

Since traditional schools followed mostly left-brain techniques, the outline was the method of choice used by most instructors. That was back in the days when most subjects were taught in a left-brain manner. We are more enlightened today—right? The people who did well in the outline technique of taking notes happened to be the left-brain students. It was the right-brain students who struggled with outlining because they do not think in a linear way.

Outlining involves listing each key point followed by the details that elaborate on that point. Those details may have further elaboration in the form of examples. One example of an outline looks like this:

Title

I. Key point
  A. Detail
    1. Example
    2. Example
  B. Detail
    1. Example
    2. Example
  C. Detail
II. Key point
  A. Detail

B. Detail
C. Detail
1. Example
2. Example

To take notes, the learner would read a paragraph using their experiential reading comprehension and memory techniques to match their superlink learning style and brain style. After they have totally understood the passage, they will recall the main idea and its details. Then, reflect on what the main idea and the details were, and insert them into their outline format as shown above. The learner should write the key point and key words for each detail from memory so they can internalize what they read. If they involve their thinking process by picking out the most important ideas and then the details and examples to support them, it reinforces their memory. The learner should not mindlessly copy the text as their notes. Copying like a parrot can be done without thinking and without remembering the material.

We may have experienced times when we have performed an automatic task, such as driving, while thinking of something else and wondering how we got to the location we did because we did not remember anything on the way. In the same way, we do not want to take notes to put words on paper without thinking or having those thoughts stick in our minds. First, we want to comprehend and remember, without notes, what we did. Then we want to convert what we have already remembered into notes, giving conscious thought to what we are doing. This actively involves us in the note-taking process so that we know exactly how the notes are associated with our memory. Then, when we look back at the notes to review for a test a week or two later, the abbreviated notes will trigger the entire memory of that section.

Three Types of Rocks

Below is a sample practice reading passage that will be used to illustrate the different note-taking techniques for both left-brain and right-brain learners. First, the learner will see what this passage would look like in the left-brain outlining technique, writing the key words in an outline form.

There are three types of rocks: sedimentary, igneous, and metamorphic rocks.

These rocks can be found in various places around the world.

Sedimentary rocks are formed by sand, soil, and bits of broken rock settling on each other to form layers. They are compressed together by the pressure of the layers on top of them. Examples of sedimentary rock are sandstone and limestone.

Igneous rocks are formed by the earth's molten magma cooling and hardening to form rock. Examples of igneous rock are obsidian and granite.

Metamorphic rocks are sedimentary and igneous rocks that are melted by the earth's heat and then cooled and hardened to form a new combination. Examples of metamorphic rocks are marble and gneiss.

Outline format:

Title: Three Types of Rocks

I. Three types of rocks: sedimentary, metamorphic, and igneous

II. Sedimentary
   A. Sand, soil, broken rocks settling to form layers
   B. Compressed from pressure of layers above them
   C. Examples
      1. Sandstone
      2. Limestone

III. Igneous
   A. Formed by molten magma
   B. Rocks formed by cooling and hardening
   C. Examples
      1. Obsidian
      2. Granite
IV. Metamorphic
   A. From sedimentary and igneous melting by earth's heat
   B. New rocks formed by cooling and hardening
   C. Examples
      1. Marble
      2. Gneiss

Technique 2: Left-brain Two-column Note-taking Technique

Another note taking method that works for left-brain learners is left-brain two-column note taking. In this method, a sheet of paper is divided into two columns. The right side will be used for taking notes in a linear form as the learner reads each paragraph. The left side is used for formulating a question that is answered by the notes in the right side. They begin by reading a paragraph using experiential reading comprehension and memory using their superlink learning style and brain style. After reading the paragraph, decide what is important and write down notes using key words as if in a list. Then look over the list. Decide what topic their notes refer to and formulate a question on that topic. Thus, when he or she is finished they will have a series of questions in the left-hand column answered by the corresponding notes in the right-hand column.

Step 1: First take notes on the right-hand column using the sample passage of the rocks above, the notes would look like this:

Questions	**Answers**
	Three types of rocks: sedimentary, metamorphic, igneous
	Sedimentary—sand, soil, broken rocks settle in layers; Compressed from pressure of layers above them Ex: sandstone, limestone
	Igneous—formed by molten magma; Rocks formed by cooling and hardening Ex: obsidian; granite
	Metamorphic— Sedimentary and igneous melting by earth's heat; new rocks formed by cooling and hardening Ex: marble, gneiss

Step 2: Add questions to the left-hand column. The learner can do this after taking all the notes for that chapter or section, or as they take notes for each paragraph. It could look like this:

Three Types of Rocks

Questions	**Answers**
What are 3 types of rocks?	3 types of rocks: sedimentary, metamorphic, igneous
What is sedimentary rock?	Sedimentary—sand, soil, broken rocks settle in layers; compressed from pressure of layers above them
What are ex. of sedimentary rock?	Ex: sandstone, limestone
What is igneous rock?	Igneous—formed by molten magma; rocks formed by cooling and hardening
What are ex, of igneous rock?	Ex: obsidian; granite
What are metamorphic rocks?	Metamorphic—sedimentary with igneous melting by earth's heat; new rocks

formed
by cooling
and hardening
What are ex. Of metamorphic rock? Ex: marble,
gneiss

The two-column note-taking technique is particularly useful for studying. The learner can fold the paper from the right margin to the middle of the page to cover the answers, leaving only the questions showing. Then read the questions and see if they can answer correctly. Open the folded paper to reveal their answers and see if they covered all the points. If so, move on to the next question. If not, put a dot as a reminder to return to this question to try it again. After going through all the questions, review those that were marked with dots, erasing or crossing out the dot when he or she answers the question correctly. In this way, the learner can avoid repeating the questions they already know and concentrate on those with which they had difficulty.

Diagram:  

Right-Brain Note-Taking Technique

Linear note-taking techniques such as outlining and listing does not work well for right-brain learners. They need to see the big picture or overview first. There are several techniques that work well for right-brain learners that give them the total picture.

Technique 1: Right-brain Two-column Note-taking Technique:

There is a way that right-brain learners can benefit from two-column note-taking. The end result looks the same as the samples provided in the left-brain two-column note-taking section. The difference is in the process of arriving at the final result.

In the right-brain two-column note-taking technique, the learner first scans the chapter, looking for the key points, then list them first as questions in the left-hand column. They can find the key points by looking at the chapter headings, the subheadings, or the topics printed in bold, and any further subtopics. Sometimes a book offers an overview with key questions at the beginning of the chapter and a review or summary with key questions or points at the end of the chapter. These topics and key points will be written as questions in the left-hand column. The right side of the brain wants to know the total picture before starting a task. By searching for all the topics to be covered in a unit or chapter first, the right-brain has a mind-set in which to place the details it will read as it goes along. Thus, it begins the chapter with a total picture. Then it will read as if searching for the answers to each question. The right side of the brain now has a purpose for reading. The details it finds will then fall into place into the framework it has already established.

This process works best when the learner has a text or book in which the topics are highlighted as titles and subtitles, or printed in bold or colored type. If a right-brain learner has a choice of several books on the same topic, it is more helpful to choose one that has the chapters broken up by subtopics, bold headers, and key points to help get the overview and to make note taking easier. Sometimes, though, there are books that are pure text, paragraph after paragraph, which are not broken up by headers for topics and subtopics. These books are more difficult for right-brain learners because they have to scan each paragraph to find topics. Thus, in the passage about the three types of rocks above, without subtitles, a right-brain learner would have to skim through it. They may come up with questions that look more like this:

Questions	**Answers**
What are 3 types of rocks?	
What is sedimentary rock?	
What is igneous rock?	
What is metamorphic rock?	

After listing all the questions, they will then read and write the answers in the right-hand column. Only after writing all the responses in the right-hand column can they see how to further break their notes up further by making some more sub questions in the left-hand column. They may find that in writing the answer on the right, they see there are some examples, and they may want to add a question such as, "What are some examples of sedimentary rock?" In some cases, they may feel there is no need to add questions and will just respond to the main question on the left-hand side by using all the details on the right-hand side as one answer.

For studying, the right-brain learners can also fold the paper from the right-hand edge to the middle of the page, covering the answers. They can then ask the question from the left-hand column and try to answer them, fold back the paper to uncover the answer, and check whether they replied correctly. They can put a dot next to questions they missed and return to them later. If they get them right on the second try, they can erase the dots or cross through them until they have answered all the missed questions correctly.

Technique 2: Right-Brain Mapping Note-Taking Technique

Mapping is a note-taking technique in which the main points of a subject are drawn out to show the overview of the relationships between information. Other words for mapping are webbing or graphic organizers, etc. At one time, I would teach the mapping technique to *everyone* only to find with dismay that the left-brain learners continued to find more success in outlining or doing two-column note-taking or making lists. Left-brain people learn better by using the left-brain linear, sequential approach, while right-brain learners prefer mapping techniques.

In its simplest form mapping note-taking looks like this:

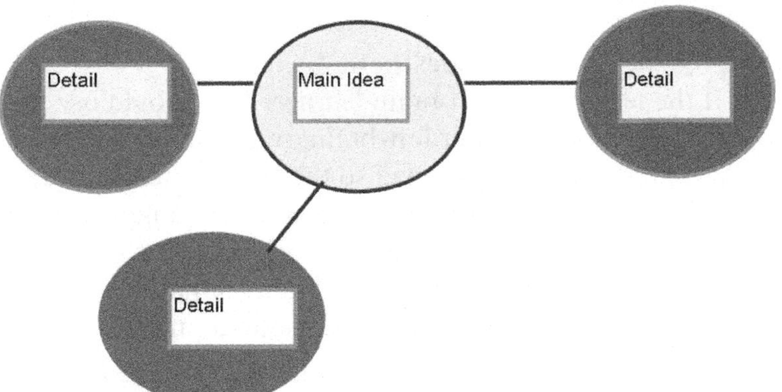

Use the same practice sample reading passage about the three types of rocks to make a map of the information. For the main idea, the learner may put in sedimentary rock. For one detail they would put in: sand, soil, broken rocks settling to form layers. For the next detail, they would put in: compressed from pressure of layers above them. For the third detail they would write: Example: sandstone, limestone.

The above map shows the relationship between the details and main idea, or subtopics and topics, so that the right side of the brain can see the global picture all at once. It is preferable that a different map be made for each new topic. If the page starts getting too crowded, the learner can make a separate map page for each main idea with its details (or each topic with its subtopics), if there are many further details or subtopics and examples.

Using the Left-Brain and Right-Brain Note-taking Skills with the Learner's Superlinks Learning Style and Brain Style

Now that you have the basic note-taking techniques for left-brain and right-brain learners, we have to adapt it for kinesthetic learners. Use the note-taking technique that fits the learner's left-brain or right-brain preference with the following additions based on their learning style:

Kinesthetic Learners

If the learner is a left-brain learner, they should use the left-brain outlining or left-brain, two-column note-taking method, using a larger pad so they can write the words larger, using their arm muscles instead of only their fine-motor finger muscles to write.

If the learner is a right-brain learner, they should use the right-brain, two-column note-taking or the right-brain map or web method, using a large size paper so they can use their arm muscles to write rather than their fine-motor finger muscles. The learner should add quick sketchy cartoon-like action pictures, diagrams, or icons, etc., alongside their notes because they will help the right-brain learner remember the action. If they are right-brain, they can use colored pens, pencils, or markers to set off the topics from the subtopics, main ideas from details, or groups of topics. They can make their map or semantic web in creative, artistic ways using different shapes and designs. Make sure their drawings are action-oriented to help them remember the notes. It is the action of drawing and writing, using their large motor muscles, that helps them remember, not necessarily seeing their notes later. They will recall what they *do*, not what they see.

Taking Notes from Verbal Presentations or Lectures, Audio-Visual Materials, Computers, Activities, and Real-Life Experiences:

If you recall, we learn not only from books and written materials, but from other forms of media as well. We may learn from verbal presentations or lectures, from audio-visual materials, computers, activities, and real-life experiences. The learner will use the same note-taking processes as described in the above sections, matching their superlink, or their brain hemispheric preference and learning style. The following adjustments need to be made for his or her learning style:

Kinesthetic Learners: Since the learner learns best by doing, they will recall activities and real-life experiences by writing a few notes, preferably in larger size on large paper, while standing up at a flip chart or white board, to trigger their memory of the event. They will find more difficulty with written materials, auditory presentations, and audio-visual materials that do not have motion. Here are some techniques to help them take notes in these situations:

1. Since the learner has already learned experiential reading comprehension and memory and how to convert written material into action in earlier chapters, their best shot is to get hold of printed material. If they are faced with an auditory presentation or lecture, get a book or textbook on the subject and read it the day or night before the lecture, taking notes from the text while standing up at a flip chart or white board. Then bring their notes to class and follow them, actively looking for material mentioned in the verbal lecture. Think of it as a

game or puzzle in which they have to find what they already wrote and add in what is new, preferably in a different color. See how many notes they took already and how many the instructor is adding. In this way, they are actively *doing* something during the lecture and will not be overwhelmed by all the talking because they already took notes in their kinesthetic style the night before.

2. If the learner cannot get hold of the text, they will have to take dictation, writing down everything the instructor says so that they can later convert it into their kinesthetic experiential reading comprehension and memory technique. Do not worry if they cannot comprehend as fast as the instructor talks—just write everything down, thinking of it as a challenge or competition to keep up with the instructor. Then convert the material into their kinesthetic note-taking approach later by going over the "transcript" of the lecture.

3. The learner should ask the instructor to provide a study guide or notes on the board that they can add to their own notes when the instructor presents anything new. This will make it easier for them to follow an auditory or audio-visual presentation.

In the exercise below, the learner should try out the note-taking techniques appropriate to their superlink, or their brain hemispheric preference and their learning style. After they find out which of the techniques they prefer, begin taking notes on the subject they selected for their field of study as they work through this book. With a little bit of practice, taking notes will become second nature and will accelerate their learning.

Exercise: Using the subject the learner is studying as they work through this book, select a passage and take notes from it using their superlink—their brain hemispheric preference and their learning style. Try both of the techniques given for their brain hemispheric preference to see which one they prefer.

Improving Study Skills

Study skills are the strategies the learner uses to review what they learned in preparation for a test or performance assessment or for using the material in real-life activities. It is a review session in which they go over the material to trigger their memory of what they already learned. In the review process they are assessing which portions of the material they know and which ones they do not know and have to relearn or clarify. One problem that many people have with study time is that this is often the *first* time they have tried to learn the material. To improve study skills, think of study as e a *review* of what has been learned, not a chance to learn something for the first time. I see many students who come to me to "study for a test," only to discover that they never learned the material in the first place. Thus, the nights before the test they are first trying to *learn* the material. If the learner finds they have to learn months of materials in hours, the best they could do the night before the exam is to use the experiential reading comprehension technique for their superlink learning style and brain style and use the memory techniques. The quantity they can study then depends on how many pages they have to cover and the time allotted to them before the test.

The learner must reframe their thoughts about studying. Do not leave the initial learning of a subject for the night before or even the week before the test. Learning must go on continually, with the appropriate method of note taking. Study time should be reserved for *reviewing* the notes that trigger what is already in their memory. Study time involves the following steps:

1. **Shorten study time by using the learner's notes to review**: If he or she takes notes, they have less to look

over than if they had to review an entire textbook. Whereas a textbook may take several hours to several days or weeks to review, the notes may take anywhere from only a few minutes to several hours.

2. **Sorting out the portions of the learner's notes that they already know from those of which they are not sure or have forgotten:** If the learner used the two-column, note-taking technique, he or she can cover up the answers on the right side of the page, ask themselves the questions on the left side of the page, and then uncover the answers to see which questions they answered correctly. Put dots next to the questions they need to review. If they used a map or semantic web approach, review what is on it, then turn the map face down and see how much of it they can recall. Put dots next to the parts of the map that they forgot and spend time going over them.

3. **Going over those portions the learner is not sure of or has forgotten:** After doing step two, the learner will be left with the questions they answered incorrectly or the parts of the map or web that they do not remember. Review them and test themselves again. If they still do not grasp them, it could be that he or she did not understand the material the first time or their notes are not clear enough to trigger their memory. In this case, he or she may have to go back to their textbook or notes of the lecture and redo that portion of their notes to make it clearer. They may have to look up some terminology in a glossary or dictionary to make it clearer. Do this until they are able to answer the question accurately.

4. **Checking the learner's understanding of the vocabulary or terminology**: The learner may want to highlight or make a separate list of terms or vocabulary he or she needs to know. The two-column approach is ideal for this because they can quiz themselves by covering up the definition. List the words in the left-hand

column and the definition in the right-hand column. Mark the words they miss and spend more time on those. They may have to make a stronger word association, as described in the chapter on memory, to help them remember better. Go over the dotted words until they get them correct.

5. **For performance tasks, do practice activities and measure the learner's performance against their goals:** In certain fields it is not so much a question of memorization of information than of performing a task or a process. Examples would be: math, chemistry, performing surgery, car repair, cooking, driving, basketball, gymnastics, construction, public speaking, writing, computer programming, or architectural design, etc. Studying for these types of performance tests means practicing the task. The learner's notes can guide them through the process, but they will have to practice to gain proficiency in it. As they do it, measure their performance against the required standards and rework those sections with which they have difficulty. The learner should have someone else help them who can guide their review and performance. The learner does not need to leave practice for the night before—enough time should be left to get help in the areas that are identified as being weak. After they get help, they need to continue to work on those portions that need improvement until they are satisfied that they meet the performance standards.

How Much Time Should You Study?

The learner needs to study until they can master the material. For some it may be minutes, for others, hours or days. A certain amount of time should not be set as the learner's goal; rather, make mastering the material as their objective. Here are some helpful hints for the learner:

1 Review the material after taking notes on it.
2. Look over the previous day's notes as a refresher before starting the current day's notes.
3. At the end of the week, review all the notes for the week.
4. At the beginning of the next week, review the previous week's notes.
5. At the end of each month, review all the notes for the past month.
6. Before the test, the learner should spend one week reviewing all their notes, section by section, so they can see all their notes at least one more time before the test.
7. The night before the test, review all notes. If time is short, review only those that they dotted as trouble spots.
8. On the morning of the test, review all the notes, or sometime during the day of the test again review the remaining dotted notes that were trouble spots.
9. If the test is not the final exam and the learner knows the material will come up again on a final examination or a qualifying, entrance, or proficiency examination, continue to review the notes once a month until the test. In the month before the test, review everything again, bit by bit. In the final week before the test, review all the dotted sections, or trouble spots, one more time. The night before the test, review all the dotted sections or trouble spots one more time.

Remember, this study time gives the learner a chance to use and retrieve what is already in their memory, keeping the memory active as long as they need it to pass a test or performance examination, or to use it on the job.

Exercise: The learner will use the notes they were taking at the beginning of this chapter for the subject they are learning, and practice studying them using the techniques described in this section. Look them over, cover them up, and see if they can recall the notes. Check their response against the written notes to see which areas they know and which they still need to study. The learner should make a timetable for themselves, entering the time of day he or she will spend daily studying the notes they have taken.

Improving Test-Taking Skills

Test-taking skills involves two steps: preparing for the test and actually taking the test. Although this section deals with traditional paper-pencil or computerized-scored tests and how to prepare for and take them, the concepts can be applied to performance assessments. While the learner's preparation may be more in the area of practice, they can prime themselves for the task by a) finding out what content is on the test and on which they will be assessed; b) practicing it; and c) understanding how their performance will be measured and what they will be expected to do at the time of assessment.

Preparing for a Test

Test preparation includes the skills we already learned: reading and/or listening comprehension, memory, note-taking skills, and study skills, plus a few additional tasks to get the learner ready for a test. If they have done their experiential reading comprehension, memory activities, and note taking, and used their appropriate study skills they have won most of the battle. However, there are a few more tasks to do to prepare for a test that are not covered by the above skills:

1. **Finding out the content on the test:** The learner may be well-prepared for what they thought would be on the test, only to discover there are items on it they did not know were going to be there. They say to themselves, "If I knew that was on the test, I would have studied for that and would have passed it." When I analyzed the test

results of students with whom I worked I find that they master everything about the topics I helped them study that was on their study to-do list. The questions they missed were only the items they did not tell me they had to study and know. The first and most important step in test preparation is to know what the test is going to cover. How can a person find that out? Easy—ask. There are two possible replies when the learner asks the instructor what is on the test: "You should know this, this, and this," which means the learner can take notes in their superlink learning style and brain style on all the items mentioned, or he or she will say, "Know everything!" in which case the learner will have to study all the written texts, class notes, and activities—everything.

Their test preparation should begin with making a chart, graph, diagram, list, semantic web or map, etc. depending on their superlink learning style and brain style, noting the items to be covered on the test.

2. **Organize the study materials**: The learner needs to organize his or her notes, lecture materials, written materials, study guides, handouts, and everything else related to each item that will be tested. Then if they find they are missing material, they have time to get it from the instructor or other participants in the class. If they missed a portion of the class, they should find out what was covered during their absence and get the materials for that section.

3. **Make a time management chart including the date and time of the test and all the time the learner has available for study:** Prepare a calendar or time management chart noting the day of the test and blocking off all the times and days the learner has available to study. Figure out how much material they need to review and study. If they took good notes they can count the number of units or sections in which their notes are

divided and determine how many they have to review before the test. Then they can decide how many units they need to study each day to reach their goal. For example:

History: Time: 3 weeks before the test or 21 days
Units: 6 units of study or 6 groups of notes needing 2 hours each 21 days divided by 6 units= 3 ½ days for each unit

This tells the learner that for each unit, he or she can spend two hours spread out over three and a half days of studying to cover all the topics before the test.

By creating calendars or time charts the learner can make sure they leave enough time to cover all the material in preparation for the test.

4. **Have the learner take a practice test simulating the actual test as closely as possible:** The learner may be perfectly prepared for the material to be tested, but are thrown off because the format of the questions is unfamiliar. For example, he or she may have been prepared for multiple-choice questions only to find that it is a fill-in-the-blank or essay test. The learner should ask in advance what the format of the test will be. Then they can do practice activities from their textbooks, work sheets, or practice pages that match the format.

5. **Know the Strategies for the Types of Test Questions:** If the learner has followed all the steps in this book so far—experiential reading comprehension, memory techniques, note-taking skills, and study skills—they should know the material thoroughly. The learner should know it as well as the instructor and have the entire textbook or course material in their head. Thus, no question should stump them because they fully understand and comprehend the subject. He or she should be able to answer a question whether it is a multiple-choice questions, fill-in-the-blank, matching,

true or false, or essay question. Even if they know the material, the format of the question has hidden pitfalls that can throw them off. They need to understand the strategies involved in answering each type of question and be prepared for them. Doing practice activities using the format that will be used on the test can prepare them so that they do not have to waste time during the test figuring out how to respond.

6. **Get in the right state of mind before the test:** If the learner thinks back to the chapter in this book on preparation for learning, he or she may recall that they need to be in a relaxed state. If they are afraid, their higher cognitive thinking centers may shut down, leaving them in the instinctive fight-or-flight part of the brain. They want to go into the test in a relaxed state so that their higher cognitive brain is working. Here are some things they can do to keep their mental attitude positive:

   a. **Relax:** Do their relaxation exercises each night during the week before the test, such as deep-breathing exercises to get the oxygen flowing to their brain. Relax their muscles. Do meditation to be in a calm and peaceful state of mind. Listen to relaxing music. Use any of the techniques that they have been using in preparation for learning.

   b. **Grow brain neurons:** Exercise and physical movement has shown to stimulate the neurotransmitters that prime brain cells for learning and reduces harmful stress. Add some physical exercise as a prelude to study time to reduce stress and fear associated with test taking. For kinesthetic learners, exercise has the added benefit since they learn best when they are moving. Combining mental tasks with physical movement helps them learn and remember faster.

c. **Visualize success:** The learner should spend a few minutes each day before the test visualizing themselves succeeding on it. See themselves answering the questions with confidence and ease. Imagine themselves getting a perfect paper. The kinesthetic learners will experience themselves standing and going up to the instructor to pick up their successful test paper and rewards.

d. **Make positive affirmations or statements** each day for a week before the test. If the learner has done all the steps described in this book, they are well prepared. Here are some examples of affirmations they can make: "I am ready for this test." "I have studied everything and know everything there is to know for this test." "I know everything that is in the book for this test." "I know everything the instructor knows for this test." "I am a good student." "I am a winner."

Taking the Test

If the learner has done all the steps laid out in this book so far, the test is actually anti-climactic. Their work is done. Their mind is filled with everything they need to know to succeed. They are in a relaxed, confident frame of mind. They have already taken the test in their mind through visualization and have passed. On the day of the test, they are merely going through the motions. The test will be a breeze because they have already learned the subject, memorized it, practiced it, reviewed it, and have their mind set to do well. They just need to remember to do the following things while taking the test:

1. Read the directions as carefully as they had studied the material, using their experiential reading comprehension. Understand each word of the directions and see, hear, feel, or experience themselves doing every step of the directions so they do not miss a word. In their mind, make a movie of themselves following the directions exactly.
2. Read each question and the choices carefully, using their experiential reading comprehension. Make a movie in their mind of what the question and choices are saying. Do not miss any details. Do not jump to conclusions. Read every word and make an image for each word. Only when they are clear about the question and choices should they proceed to answer the question.
3. Stay relaxed so they are in the higher cognitive thinking part of the brain. If they feel any fear or nervousness, take some deep breaths, exercise, or take a few seconds to meditate to stay relaxed.
4. If they find a hard question, mark a dot next to it, and return to it. Do not waste too much time on hard questions, but in each section do all the ones they know first and return to the hard questions at the end. Spending time on one hard question can cost the learner four or five shorter questions. Often, after doing the easier questions, the harder ones become easier as well.
5. Pace themselves. If there are longer questions or essay questions, decide how much time they want to spend on the shorter questions and how much time they need to leave for the longer ones. Move quickly and read every word, but do not rush. Missing important words could throw them off.

6. If there is time left over, return to check their answers. Do not haphazardly change their answers. Remember, they have thought through and analyzed their choices, so they were probably right the first time around. Only change an answer if the learner knows they guessed the first time around without analyzing. Do the analysis first, eliminating poor choices, and then change the answer only if they can prove that the new choice is the correct one.
7. Trust their memory. The learner spent a lot of time converting everything they learned into a movie or experience in their mind based on their superlink learning style and brain style. Their memory in their best learning style and brain style is excellent. When they rerun those memories in their learning style and brain style, the answers are there. Trust them.

Exercise:

Option 1: If the learner is taking a course concurrently in the subject that they are using to work through the book, use the techniques in this chapter to prepare for a test if one is scheduled.

Option 2: If they are not currently taking a course that has a test, find a book or workbook on the subject that they are studying that has a practice test, chapter review check-up, or a quiz. Use it as a practice test for this exercise. See what is on the test and do the activities in this chapter to prepare for the "test."

For both Option 1 and Option 2: Make a timetable for studying for the test. Fix the date for the test, analyze how much material the learner needs to review, and then fill in the calendar. The learner should get used to doing this for upcoming tests so that they leave themselves enough time to study. Remember, study time is there for *reviewing* what the student has already learned—not for first *learning* the subject!

The learner now knows the secrets of how to learn anything quickly and accurately.

BONUS SECTION: KINESTHETIC RIGHT-BRAIN LEARNER ACTIVITIES and COPING STRATEGIES

CHAPTER 8: ACTIVITIES AND COPING STRATEGIES TO HELP KINESTHETIC RIGHT-BRAIN LEARNERS READ, COMPREHEND, REMEMBER, AND LEARN

Having a kinesthetic right-brain learning preference can be an asset to learning quickly. Since their goal is to do things rapidly, they will maximize their skills and assets to reach goals quicker. Any subject can be learned by a kinesthetic right-brain learner if taught in their Superlink learning and brain style.

Here are activities and coping strategies for a kinesthetic right-brain learner to be able to accelerate reading, comprehension, remembering, and learning anything quickly, by converting it into their kinesthetic right-brain style of learning. This chapter contains many coping strategies for the kinesthetic right-brain learner to take any material that is not in his or her Superlink style and convert it to his or her best and fastest way of learning.

Activities to Try

Activity: Converting Printed Written Material for the Kinesthetic

Right-brain Learner: Kinesthetic right-brain learners do not think in terms of words and numbers. They process stimulus in the form of concrete, sensory experiences. They also require movement. Thus, they need to go through a process to convert written material into their kinesthetic right-brain Superlink learning style. If they cannot physically act out what they are reading, they can convert the words into an action movie in their head. They should become the director and make a video production on the screen. For each phrase read, have them describe, "What is on my movie screen now?" They can either have the characters on their screen act out the movements, or they can become the actors or actresses and experience themselves doing the action. This is a perfect opportunity to involve their imagination. Within the parameters of the descriptions written on the page, they can add their own imaginative touch. Thus, with one swoop they have converted abstract words on a page into the kinesthetic movement with a right-brain concrete movie experience. If the text is written in a detailed manner, have them convert each detail into another scene of their movie. Help them pay attention to time order words in the text by having them associate it with an actual time of day in which they "do" something in their daily lives. What action does he or she do during that time of day? Have him or her connect their own action with the time words in the story to help them remember it. This can be done for everything they read.

Example: If the learner is reading about a blood cell in the body, they can imagine being the blood cell. They can feel themselves racing through the freeways of the body's veins, dropping off oxygen and picking up carbon dioxide, carrying nutrients, and expelling wastes. If they become that blood cell and feel the action, they can learn the role of those cells in the body. If they are learning about verbs, they should act out the verb and feel themselves doing that action.

There is no limit to the amount of kinesthetic activities they can do to convert the written word into action for whatever they need to learn. I have created an entire K-12 and college curriculum of reading and learning activities for kinesthetic right-brain learners, of which I have given hundreds of examples in this book, so it is possible to take any of their schoolwork that is written and convert it into kinesthetic right-brain activities.

Activity: Mind Mapping Written Material

You can also take the written material and have the learner write the global or main ideas in a mind map format, so they can get the big picture of what they are reading. Involve their muscles by having them make the mind map by writing on large sheets of paper hung on the wall or on a flip chart.

Activity: Move While Reading

Another activity is to have the learner move while they read. Many kinesthetic right-brain people find it more comfortable to read stretched out on a couch, an easy chair, or carpet. Then, they have room to stretch and move their legs freely on the floor or couch. Have them hold the book above their head. Some people like to walk across the room while they read. Others pedal on an exercise bike. If the written material is mounted on a wall or board, they can jump rope or jog while reading. Some people mount it on their kitchen window and read while washing the dishes.

Activity: Make a Game Out of Reading

The child or teen can play games as they read. For every sentence or paragraph, have them toss a ball into a basket, throw a ring in a ring toss game, dance to the music, or give themselves a snack break. Competitions with themselves in which they try to beat their own record is another incentive to keep the reading action oriented.

Activity: Eliminate Distractions

Since action of others moving around can distract a kinesthetic right-brain learner (not their own actions!), block off their view of other activities through the use of a room divider or screen. Do not allow them to watch television while they read written material, but use the television, or music, or another relaxing activity as a reward to break up the reading period. (If a parent does not permit television in the house, then have the learner do another recreational activity as a reward for every certain amount of minutes they did their schoolwork or homework.) Some kinesthetic right-brain learners can work with rhythmic music. Parents can make a reward system for the learner; for example, for every half hour they read, they get a half hour of television, listening to music, or another activity they like.

The more movement that the learner can connect with reading in some way, the more their best learning modality is opened. Their stress is reduced because they are comfortable with the movement. With lowered stress, their higher cognitive functions can concentrate on learning.

Activity: Converting Printed Graphic Material for the Kinesthetic Right-brain Learner

Graphic material can be easily understood by the right side of the brain, but the kinesthetic right-brain learner needs to do something with it. He or she can build or construct something based on the graphic material. They can dramatize the material in some active way. They can set up a circumstance with three-dimensional objects to demonstrate the relationships shown on the graphics. By taking the labels on a printed graphic chart and putting them on large index cards or three-dimensional objects and moving them around on the floor or a wall, they can actively recreate the graphic. They can take photographs and illustrations and make them come alive by turning them into movies in their mind. They can take a map, and walk in the direction they would travel on the map, turning where the map has them turn. The key is to involve their muscles in some way in bringing the graphic to life to help them grasp it.

Activity: Converting Audio-Visual Material for the Kinesthetic Right-brain Learner

Action on the screen is their best audio-visual media. Movies, videos, and television are the best audio-visual materials, but only second to them actual moving themselves. A kinesthetic right-brain learner requires frequent change. They prefer quick-moving programs that present the big picture, not a lot of sequential details. Have them convert stationary slides, power points, and filmstrips by having them do an action to accompany it or mentally imagine themselves doing the action in their mind.

Activity: Converting Audio Material for the Kinesthetic Right-brain Learner

Audio material containing verbal presentations on CD's, digital audio files, or radio will also need to be converted into a movie in their mind. If there is music in them, they can move to the rhythm and beat.

As they watch the action on video, DVD or other media with audio-visual presentations, they may find themselves moving in time to the music or along with the characters, with their body swaying, gyrating, bouncing, jumping, or doing the silent cheer with their arms. Try to select audio-visual materials that come with activity kits and projects they can do. If not, let them use their vivid imagination and create their own. If at all possible, have manipulative materials in front of them as they watch or listen so they can do the project simultaneously with the program. Think of different ways they can make a project out of the materials. This will increase their ability to learn.

Activity: Watch and Do

Find some audio-visual material on a topic they need to learn for school. Have them do a real-life activity with movement involved to accompany the audio-visual. They do not need step-by-step directions. They can just jump in and do it along with the audio-visual material, because they can pick up the global overview of what is happening. Their body can instinctively do the action that others do, even without words and directions.

Activity: Converting Information from Computers for the Kinesthetic Right-brain Learner

Learning from computers is good for kinesthetic right-brain people if the software contains high action with free-flowing, creative interaction. That is why many kinesthetic right-brain people like computer games. They want spontaneous action in which they can respond quickly with their instincts. If it is not high action and interactive, conversions to the correct learning style will need to be made.

If the software contains words in the form of written text or audio, they have to either do actions along with it or turn the language into a movie in their head. If the software contains still graphics, they have to visualize themselves putting into action what the graphics is showing and enact their movements in their mind. If the software is sequential, try to skip through to find the key points, summary, or main idea, and work on those.

Activity: Keyboard Challenge

Using a mouse or a joystick is more simultaneous and kinesthetic than typing on a keyboard in a linear, step-by-step way. If they must type, let them challenge themselves to increase their speed, competing with their previous record.

Activity: Kinesthetic Online Courses

If a kinesthetic right-brain learner is learning through an online course, then the material presented should guide them to do activities where they get up and move. Although the computer program or Internet course or e-course is going to present something visually on the screen with graphics, or voice, the key is that the instructions should be guiding them to get up and engage in kinesthetic activities to learn in between the given instructions. Building in goals in which they win points towards prizes also converts the activity into a kinesthetic one.

Activity: Converting Learning Activities for the Kinesthetic Right-brain Learner

Movement activities are one of the best ways for a kinesthetic right-brain person to learn so no conversion is generally needed. Experiments, exploration, discovery, role-playing, simulations, learning games and projects allow their body to move. These movement activities provide freedom of choice, options, and imagination. Kinesthetic right-brain people with their absence of a sense of time can get entranced by a project and often stay engaged for long periods of time. When they enjoy something they lose track of time, often working long past the stopping time.

Activity: Converting Visual, Auditory, or Tactile Activities to Movement

If the activities are mostly visual, they must convert them into action by making the product. If this is not possible, let them imagine themselves making it in their mind. It is important that they feel the movements of their body as they visualize. If the activities are auditory, they need to act out the descriptions with their body, or feel themselves doing it in their mind. If there are tactile activities, they can carry out the task by standing up or doing them on a larger scale to involve the body. Find imaginative and novel ways to carry out the task.

Strategy: Converting Learning from Real-Life Experiences for the Kinesthetic Right-brain Learner

Real-life experiences offer kinesthetic right-brain people an ideal learning experience so no conversion is needed for these. They can jump in and get involved. This allows the learners to be a part of on-the-job training, apprenticeships, and participation in real-life situations rather than just reading or hearing about it. It offers the right side of their brain a chance to get the whole picture or overview of a task as performed in its authentic setting. They have a chance to involve their senses to experience the sights, sounds, smells, tastes, and feelings of the happening. Opportunities to use their imagination or inventiveness are preferable. They often see new and better ways of doing things. They can offer their talents to exploring new approaches.

If the real-life experience involves mostly the visual or auditory sense, have them act out doing the task, or imagine their body doing the task in their mind. If the real-life experience involves the tactile sense, they should try to carry it out standing up, moving around, or imagine doing it in their mind kinesthetically.

If the learner finds the real-life experience is a step-by-step process, they should ask for the whole picture or bottom line first. Then the steps will make sense to them in the overall context.

The main coping skill to be alert to is harnessing their characteristic of being holistic when faced with a situation that requires sequential organization or rules and regulations. Also, their lack of time and linear organization may be perceived by others as carelessness, laziness, or rebelliousness. In real-life situations that involve organization of materials or work flow or that demand that they stick to a schedule, kinesthetic right-brain people have a difficult time. They may have to adjust to the situation by forcing themselves, with all the energy at their command, to save their imagination and freedom for another circumstance. It almost seems unfair that they have to work doubly harder than most other Superlinks learning styles to fit in. It is as hard for them to stick to routines, schedules, staying still, looking, and listening, as it would be for a visual person to work in an environment in which there was nothing to look at, or an auditory person in an environment in which no listening, talking, or discussion is allowed. Until more arrangements are made to accommodate the kinesthetic right-brain Superlinks learning style in the visual, auditory, and tactile, left-brain workaday world, the greatest burden is put on them to conform. They often have to stifle who they are for the sake of maintaining their position, until they can choose for themselves. This is a tough burden to bear, and many kinesthetic right-brain people cannot harness their need to move, need to be free to make choices, need to use their imagination, and need to use their ability to think and do many tasks at the same time. Others may think the kinesthetic right-brain person has a choice in the matter, but the choice is not in their hands--it is the way they are constructed. It is their Superlink learning style and they cannot help the way they are. As long as they can understand these strong compelling needs of their learning style, then they can try to communicate their characteristics to others to help them understand them as a whirlwind of energy, change, and creativity.

Activity: Converting Learning Information from a Person for the Kinesthetic Right-brain Learner

Kinesthetic right-brain learners take in information best from a person who allows them freedom of movement, no physical restraints, no mental restraints, free use of their imagination, tolerance for their lack of time or lack of sequential organization, and understanding of their simultaneous thinking that causes them to jump from one thought to another because they see interconnections well. Their associative thinking causes them to change the topic frequently, sometimes in the middle of a sentence to something else they have thought of related to the current point. It seems like they have an attention problem because they may change the subject in the middle of a conversation or they may drop one project for a new one suddenly. They can do many projects simultaneously and may move back and forth from one to the other like quick-moving mercury. Thus, they need to learn from a person who can understand the kinesthetic right-brain learners' needs lest they get labeled as being hyperactive, uncontrollable, or having an attention-deficit disorder such as ADHD or ADD. Many students who have a kinesthetic right-brain learning preference come under observation as having ADHD or ADD or attention-deficit disorder and even get put on medication when in actuality they may merely be kinesthetic right-brain learners. Until society recognizes this type of Superlinks learning style and brain style and provides learning experiences compatible with their needs, they remain highly misunderstood and often put at risk because they do not fit in with the system. If they have an instructor who understands them and can teach them in their kinesthetic right-brain style, their innate abilities will surface and they can accelerate their learning phenomenally. Many "gifted" people did not fit into the structure of academic learning environments, yet used their genius to make a profound contribution to humanity. Albert Einstein did poorly in school, yet the flight of his right-brain imagination intuited the theory of relativity, which led to a revolutionary transformation of life on our planet. There are many brilliant people hidden in the personages of many a kinesthetic right-brain person--it requires a person to teach them who understands them to tap into it.

If kinesthetic right-brain learners find themselves being taught by a visual person, then they should use their imagination to devise a project in which they can bring to life the visual material in an active, movement oriented way. They can do so by imagining the action or try to role-play the situation. If kinesthetic right-brain learners are being taught by an auditory person, they need to physically carry out the directions or imagine themselves doing so with their body. If kinesthetic right-brain learners are being taught by a tactile person, they should try to do the hands-on activities standing up, moving around, or producing it in a larger size to involve their body. Writing on a flip chart or a white board helps them to stand up and use their arm muscles. If a step-by-step approach in any of the modalities is required, then the kinesthetic right-brain learners need to ask the teacher to give them the bottom line or the big picture first, and then go back and fill in the steps.

If the situation is too constrained, the kinesthetic right-brain learner may end up gravitating to subjects or jobs in which they have freedom of movement and thought. They may find themselves in outdoor jobs, traveling positions, artistic fields, sports, exploration, invention, making discoveries, designing, creative endeavors, and any job that allows free movement. No matter where they are, the kinesthetic right-brain learners needs to look for coaches, facilitators, or instructors who also have a right-brained preference or understands how to teach through right-brained techniques or the kinesthetic right-brain learners may be frustrated and constrained being taught with a sequential approach.

As long as the kinesthetic right-brain learner can add movement to whatever the person instructing them wants them to do, they can stay on task and be focused. Their attention, then, will be glued to the project and others will see how productive and hard-working they really are. Their natural talents will be recognized as they use the kinesthetic energy of their body to learn and develop.

Personal Worksheet

Activity: List coping strategies from this chapter that you plan on using with the learner to convert material taught through other Superlinks styles into their own kinesthetic right-brain style:

Activities to Try

Strategy: Teaching Reading

Activity Examples of Teaching Reading Skills to a Kinesthetic Right-brain Learner

Here are more examples from my Keys to reading Success program that teaches pre-K, K-12, and college reading skills in comprehension, phonics, vocabulary, fluency, and test prep to show how reading skills can be taught to kinesthetic right-brain learners. Included is an example of a phonics skill and a comprehension skill to give an idea of how these skills can be taught to a kinesthetic right-brain person.

Strategy: Teaching a Phonics Skill to a Kinesthetic Right-brain Learner:

Activity: Superlinks™ to Teaching Consonant Blends:

Step 1: Select a consonant blend such as "bl" and have the learner copy you in writing the two letters in the air with his or her writing arm. While writing it in the air, the learner should say the letter and conclude with making the whole sound of "bl" as in "blue."

Step 2: Then, have the learner write the letter in large size in colored marker while standing up at a flip chart. After writing bl, and saying it, have the learner draw an action picture that starts with "b."

Step 3: Next, have the learner use large size three-dimensional letter blocks for "b" and "l" with the rest of the letters of the alphabet. Have them add letters to "bl" to make words.

Step 4: Have the learner do an action that starts with the letters "bl" and say the sound "bl" as they do the action.

Step 5: As they say the sound of the consonant blend "bl," followed by words that start with the blend (blend), have them throw a ring in a ring toss game or do some fun movement activity with their body. Give them points for each time they read the word and throw the ring on the target in the ring toss game or whatever physical activity they selected to do for fun. Reward them with points toward a reward. Have the learner play games like these to learn the other consonant blend patterns.

When kinesthetic right-brain learners learn phonics, or letter-sound relationships, through their preferred Superlinks learning style, learning is accelerated, easier, and more fun because they are working in their element.

Strategy: Teaching a Comprehension Skill to a Kinesthetic Right-brain Learner

Activity: Superlink™ to Find the Time Order or Sequence in a Passage:

One type of comprehension task based on literal information is time order or sequence. This involves putting events of a text, whether fiction or nonfiction, in chronological order, time order, or in sequence. Sometimes it deals with deciding what happened first, second, third, or last. At other times it involves taking events that are listed out of order and putting them back in order. The following is an example of a lesson that helps a kinesthetic right-brain learner (which means they do not think sequentially or in chronological order) learn the skill in their own Superlink style.

Step 1: Select a fiction story from the learner's schoolwork or homework or a reading-for-fun book. Give him or her large strips of poster board or newsprint. Have him or her write on each strip while standing up or stretching out each event of the story and illustrate with fast action cartoon drawings the events.

Step 2: Mix up the strips out of order. Then, have him or her lay the event strips on the floor in the order in which they happened. Then, have them move from one to the other, looking at the cartoon and acting it out to make a connection between the time order of events with their muscle movement. **Note:** The order should be correct, but the strips can be placed on the floor in a nonlinear way, such as squiggly lines, a large circle, or diagonally, right to left or left to right, etc.

Personal Worksheet

Activity: List reading strategies from this chapter that you plan on using with the learner:

Activity to Try

Strategy: Kinesthetic Right-brain Superlinks™ Memory Technique

Activity: Kinesthetic Right-brain Words: In many school subjects, one has to remember information. In science, one may be required to learn the Periodic Table of Elements. In social studies, one may need to learn the states of a country or important dates in history. In literature, one may need to memorize the important characters in a story. Here is an example activity to help a kinesthetic right-brain learner remember a list of words. The learner can apply this technique to remember material in any school subject!

Example word list: cat, house, moon, apple, football

Step 1: Tell the kinesthetic right-brain learner to imagine acting out a story with each word from the example word list. Have him or her feel his or her muscles going through the motions associated with each word. The kinesthetic right-brain learner will connect the words to an action, but does not need to do so in the order given. The kinesthetic right-brain learner does not think in a linear, sequential way and can remember them in any order he or she wants.

Example movements for the word (but let him or her think of his or her own):

1) He or she acts like a cat by crawling around the floor.
2) He or she acts as if building a house. Outside

the house, he or she imagines building a playground, and then plays on the equipment.
3) He or she is flying in a space ship to the moon, and then hopping around the moon.
4) He or she is twirling an apple and tossing it up and down in the air.
5) He or she is catching a football and run to the goal line to make a touchdown.

Now, have him or her replay the action imagined and repeat the five words aloud, in any order!

Personal Worksheet

Activity: List the memory strategy from this chapter that you plan on using with the learner in his or her kinesthetic right-brain style.

How a Kinesthetic Right-brain Learner Can Learn Anything Quickly

For the past thirty-nine years I have been teaching people of all ages how to learn any subject quickly. Kinesthetic right-brain learners can also learn anything quickly. Here are some strategies to help a kinesthetic right-brain learner convert any subject delivered in his or her non-preferred Superlink style and convert it into his or her preferred Superlink learning style.

How to Convert Input Delivered in Your Weaker Learning Styles into the Learner's Own Best Style

As the instructor, you now have some understanding of the way instruction can be delivered so that a kinesthetic right-brain learner can accelerate learning. You know the medium in which the material should be conveyed, the best materials, and the best environment for learning. So far so good. If you are the parent, you could help the teacher or educator teach in the way that will help your child or teen learn quickly. However, we do not always have control over the different factors. We may not be the ones in charge of getting the information conveyed through the best medium. We cannot always be in control of choosing the material. The learning environment is not always in our control. Is it hopeless? No, not at all. What you *can* do is convert any input into your child's best style. Your child can still learn, even if the medium, material, and environment does not suit his or her preferred Superlink style if they are converted. The following are coping skills to help convert any input into your child's or teen's own Superlink style. Think of it as a translation system.

Let us suppose the instructor or trainer does not convey information in the medium that is best for your child and has selected materials that does not match his or her kinesthetic right-brain Superlink style. Further, let us suppose that the learning environment is not compatible with your child's best style. Here is what you can do to turn a poor situation into an optimal one.

Activity: Converting the Medium and Materials into the Child's or Teen's Kinesthetic Right-brain Superlink

Directions: In the following chart, the child or teen's best Superlink is listed on the left side. Listed across the top are different media in which information is conveyed. Where the two intersect, you will find an asterisk (*) indicating that that is the correct media for you to use. If it is not the correct media, instructions on how to convert it into his or her best media is given.

Converting Printed Written Material for a Kinesthetic Right-Brain Learner

Activity

<u>Printed Written Material</u>

Conversion: The learner needs to act out the words or imagine the action in his or her mind.

<u>Printed Graphic Material</u>
Conversion: The learner needs to physically act out the graphic representation or imagine the action in his or her mind.

<u>Audio-Visual Material</u>
Activity: Ideal for watching action on video, movies, television or animations. The learner imagines themselves doing the action.
Conversion: Slides, filmstrips need to be dramatized or action needs to be imagined in the mind.

<u>Computers</u>
Activity: Ideal for high-action computer programs that are interactive; interactive electronic communication and virtual reality.
Conversion: Written text or graphics on computers need to be acted out or action imagined in the mind.

<u>Activities</u>
Activity: Ideal for activities involving movement, freedom of movement, and imagination.
Conversion: Visual, auditory, and tactile activities need to be acted out or action imagined in the mind.

<u>Real-Life Experience</u>
Activity: Ideal for real-life experiences involving movement with freedom of movement and imagination.
Conversion: Visual, auditory and tactile real-life experiences need to be acted out or action imagined in the mind with freedom of movement and imagination.

<u>Learning from a Person</u>
Activity: Ideal if instructor provides movement activities, freedom of movement, and imagination.
Conversion: For visual, auditory and tactile instructors, need to act out or imagine action in the mind with freedom of movement and imagination.

More Resources for Kinesthetic Right-brain Learners:

Activity: To find out how to apply the learner's particular Superlink to learning anything quickly, select the topic you need from the list below to move on to other books, materials, trainings, and courses in our series for kinesthetic learners. These skills can help improve reading, memory, and learning in any content area whether science, social science, health, literature, health, a language, or any academic or vocational topic that involves reading or studying. Mastering kinesthetic reading will be an asset to learning any subject.

Enjoy the dramatic difference these skills will make as the kinesthetic right-brain learner applies kinesthetic techniques to be the best in any subject they want to master!

They can have fun learning as they reach their goals in life!

BONUS SECTION: KINESTHETIC LEFT-BRAIN LEARNERS ACTIVITIES and COPING STRATEGIES

CHAPTER 9: ACTIVITIES AND COPING STRATEGIES TO HELP KINESTHETIC LEFT-BRAIN LEARNERS READ, COMPREHEND, REMEMBER AND LEARN

The techniques for kinesthetic left-brain learning can be applied to read, comprehend, remember, and learn any subject. Kinesthetic left-brain learners can apply their particular Superlink learning style to learn anything quickly.

In the educational system today, reading forms the base of learning most subjects. Take any course and there is bound to be some work required in reading the words of the text fluently, comprehending it, and studying for tests. Once kinesthetic left-brain learners decide their goals, they can learn how to apply the kinesthetic left-brain strategies to learn any subject.

Here are activities and coping strategies for a kinesthetic left-brain learner to accelerate reading, comprehension, remembering, and learning anything quickly, by converting it into their kinesthetic left-brain style of learning. This chapter contains many coping strategies for kinesthetic left-brain learners so they can convert any material not in their preferred Superlink™ style into his or her own best and quickest way of learning.

Activities to Try

Activity: Converting Printed Written Material for the Kinesthetic Left-brain Learner: Kinesthetic left-brain learners like things presented in the form of words and numbers. They also like things presented sequentially.

But they cannot just look at words; they need to do something active with them. They do well with step-by-step instructions for movement activities. They end up reading guides while performing the tasks to playing baseball, basketball, golf, using a computer, building a house, planting a tree farm, laying brick, driving a race car, etc. They like written material that is action oriented which directs them to carry out the actions. If they read about how someone climbed a mountain, they want to go out and try it, too. If the material does not contain action it will put them right to sleep. They will tune out or rush through it, barely paying attention to what it says.

Here are some conversion techniques to deal with material that is not action oriented. First, they have to realize that books were written to put down on paper some life activity or process. The words may seem lifeless, but the words were actually a screenplay depicting an aspect of life that someone decided to write down. The only way they are going to survive is to convert the words back into live action. For this, they need to make a movie out of it. They should treat each piece of written material as a screenplay for a video movie. It is their job to stage the lights, camera, and action. They can do this in one of two ways: They can physically enact what they are reading; or they can imagine themselves doing the action in their mind. They must feel themselves moving along with the content described in the text. For example, if they are reading about the water cycle, they can feel themselves move like a water droplet being sucked up into the sky. They can then imagine themselves being packed together with other water droplets in a cloud. Next, they can imagine being knocked around by condensation. Finally, they can imagine free-falling back down to the ground as rain. Wheeeee! Fun, isn't it! As kinesthetic left-brain learners the way the action is imaged should be as a step-by-step process, which is ideal for them. They can do this with any subject: for example, in math—they can become the numbers and act out a situation related to the math problem. In social studies, they can become an explorer during the fifteenth century traveling the seas to new lands. In learning about auto mechanics, they can become the piston in the engine. If learning quantum physics, then imagine moving in a particle accelerator. This method is more movement oriented and fun than just reading words on a page without converting it into action.

Activity: Action Notes: Another method is for the kinesthetic left-brain learner to take notes in large size, while standing. This involves their muscles. They can write on a flip chart, chalkboard, or chart paper using large markers and their entire arm muscles. They can make a step-by-step chart of the materials. While writing, they should use the muscles of their arm rather than the fine motor muscles of the fingers to push the hand and pencil or markers. This will get their arm more actively involved.

Activity: Cut Down Distractions: If there is a lot of activity around a kinesthetic left-brain learner that distracts them from reading, put up a divider or screen to block out their view of others' actions. Try to impress upon their instructor their need to move so they can do their writing at a board or flip chart.

Activity: Comfort Work: The simple act of standing up, or stretching out comfortably on a sofa or reclining chair helps their body have freedom to move and wiggle around as they read. Some people read well by walking back and forth, lying on their back, holding the book up over their head, or sitting on an exercise bike and pedaling while they read. They need to find some way to make the situation tolerable for them. Their facility to take in information is highest when their body is moving.

Activity: Movement Goals: When reading on their own, they need to set movement goals for themselves. For every paragraph they read, allow them to shoot a ball into a basket or waste paper basket. They can squeeze or bounce a ball as they read. They can get up and "act out" the material with their body as they read.
Activity: Beat Your Record: Have the learner start some kind of competition going with himself or herself to make it a game situation. For example, have him or her earn a reward of taking a walk or snack break for each chapter they read or each problem they do. Set a timer and have him or her race against his or her own record to see how much can be accomplished within that time limit. As long as they keep moving, their distractions will be lessened. The key is to combine movement with reading in some way so that their best learning mode is open. Without movement, they become stressed out and their higher cognitive functions can shut down as their instinctive survival needs to rid themselves of the stress is activated. Reducing stress for them is through movement.
Activity: Converting Printed Graphic Material for the Kinesthetic Left-brain Learner: A kinesthetic left-brain learner needs to do something with the graphic material in order to learn. They may need to physically act out the relationships illustrated in the graphic material. In their mind they can convert the graphic material into a movie and imagine themselves as part of the action. This medium requires a double conversion for them, because the left side of the brain is word oriented. They may have to first analyze the graphic material and convert it into step-by-step words, and then enact the movie in their head. They may want to make a three-dimensional model in a step-by-step way to represent the graphic material. Moving large objects and hands-on manipulatives can help them portray what is in the

material. They can also copy the diagram or chart on a large poster or flip chart, using their large muscles.

If the graphics are too holistic for them and they cannot grasp the sequential steps in it, have them learn to ask questions to get the points they need to understand explained by their instructor.

Activity: From Maps to Directions: When they read maps, they tend to best perceive the words and the compass direction between the places. As they make step-by-step directions to get from one place to another, they should imagine themselves moving along that route, feeling their body turn right or left at the appropriate places. They need to experience themselves driving in a car and turning at certain landmarks along the way, feeling their body shift right or left as the turns are made.

Activity: Converting Audio Visual Material for the Kinesthetic Left-brain Learner: Of all the audio-visual media, the best for kinesthetic left-brain learners are those that shows action on the screen. The still photographs in filmstrips and slides engage them if they show action poses. There is just not enough happening. The best formats, though, for them are movies, video, MP4s, and television in which they can watch the action while getting up and doing activities along with it. Of course, *doing* the action is the best. If they cannot perform the action, watching it is second best. If you observe a kinesthetic left-brain person watching television or video, you may see their body move along with the action. You may see their bodies turn to the right and left as they watch a racing car veer around the track, or they may lift up an arm as if to shoot a ball into a net along with the player on the screen. Hitting their hand into their fist may accompany a boxing punch on the screen. This behavior does not only hold true for kinesthetic learners who are sports-minded people. Kinesthetic left-brain learners can like other action oriented happenings as well. When watching a gourmet cook on television, the kinesthetic left-brain learner may stir an imaginary pot along with the person on the screen.

Kinesthetic left-brain people prefer sequential and detailed presentations. Sports with rules and regulations, step-by-step methods, and how-to shows such as how to build a house, bake bread, dance, or do a science experiment all involve watching the steps to perform an action.

It would be best if kinesthetic left-brain learners could do the action along with any audio-visual presentation. They should stand up and do the moves along with the program. Exercise or dance videos will work for them if they can do it along with the program. Learning an instrument is best when they can play along with the audio-visual instructions. Learning to use a computer software program should be both done on a computer while watching or listening to the presentation.

If it not possible to do the action while watching or listening to audio-visual material, what they should do is to experience themselves doing the action in their mind along with the presentation. They should imagine themselves carrying out the movements in the order in which they are given.

Another strategy is that the kinesthetic left-brain learners draw out the moves conveyed by the audio-visual material on a large poster, white board, or flip chart, while standing up and use large motor arm muscles to illustrate the movements being described in the video, movie, photo, or audiotape.

Audio-visual materials with worksheets, study guides, or activity sheets in which they can do something to accompany what they learned and which are sequential help kinesthetic left-brain learners. Many DVD, MP4, or video series, or instructional movies come with a workbook or study guide. Select those that have follow-up activities that they can do. Note that activities come in many shapes and sizes. They can be real-life simulations and experiences in which they can engage to act out or perform the material. Performing real-life activities falls is kinesthetic if movement is involved. If it is presented in a step-by-step way, it is ideal for them.

Activity: Nutrition in Motion: Select a topic about health and nutrition from the child or teen's health or biology book. Have the learner make a large size poster charting his or her daily diet. Have him or her then research the vitamins and minerals contained in the food he or she eats each day. Have him or her list on the chart how much each food contains and analyze whether he or she is getting enough of each. Have him or her put out the boxes or wrappers for the food to see the mineral and vitamin content. Then, have him or her make an action plan to make sure he or she is getting enough of these vitamins and minerals. He or she can set a goal, and keep a daily chart, putting on stickers or reward himself or herself for sticking with the plan.

Activity: Converting Audio Material for the Kinesthetic Left-brain Learner: Straight audio as in audiotapes, CD's, MP3s, and radio can be made action oriented, if there are mostly action words, for example, as is found in the broadcasting of a sports events, and they guide the kinesthetic left-brain learner to do action activities, movements, or real-life simulations. Since information has to be conveyed in some way, if it is auditory with action words it needs to guide the kinesthetic left-brain learner to get up and move.

Audio materials that come with worksheets, study guides, or activity sheets in which they can do something to accompany what they learned helps them. Find audiotape, CD, or MP3 series that have a workbook. Those that have follow-up activities they can do and are sequential are helpful. The activities can be real-life experiences in which they can engage to accompany the material. Doing a real-life activity also falls into the realm of being kinesthetic if there is movement involved.

Activity: From Sound to Motion: Have the learner select an audio or MP3 about a subject he or she wants to learn for fun. Have him or her act out the instructions from the MP3 while listening and actually do the activities it directs him or her to do.

Activity: Converting Information from Computers for the Kinesthetic Left-brain Learner: Learning from computers is good for kinesthetic left-brain people if the software contains actions to be performed in a step-by-step way. There are many computer games or interactive programs that involve action in which the learner follows a sequence of moves. Instructional software is also excellent if it guides the kinesthetic left-brain learners through steps to engage in action leading to learning a subject.

If the software is just text, or text and audio, it is better if action words are used to convey activity. The text or audio plus text can be used if it guides the kinesthetic left-brain learner to get up, move, and do something with the information. However, if it has no instructions leading to some action or no action words, they will have to convert what they read into action in an imaginary movie they make in their mind. If it is action, but too global, they may have to write it out in step-by-step format first and then try to make sense of it.

Using a mouse or a joystick is more active than typing. The Kinesthetic left-brain can handle typing because of their facility with words and numbers. It should just be more interactive such as in a game or challenge format or guide them to do activities.

A computer program gives them step-by-step instructions that they can use to act out in real life is the best. Just watching without getting up and doing the action along with it is not movement-oriented enough for them.

Virtual reality in which they are part of the action is great if they can follow it in a step-by-step way. Without step-by-step guidance, the experience is too holistic and simultaneous that they may become lost; thus, they need to get systematic help from someone before entering that fast-action, moving world.

Activity: Step-by-Step Webinar in Motion: Have the learner use a webinar or video that is step-by-step to learn a subject and enact the instructions by standing up and doing the motions described. Select one with step-by-step instructions.

Activity: Online Courses for Kinesthetic Learners: Have the learner take an online courses that is step-by-step in a subject in which he or she needs help and use the strategies to convert the audio and/or video from the course into action.

Activity: Converting Information from Learning Activities for the Kinesthetic Left-brain Learner: Kinesthetic left-brain learners are in their element when they are doing step-by-step activities. Getting involved in projects that involve their body, such as experiments, discovery, role-playing, learning games, and simulations, are ideal.

If the activities are mostly visual, they need to convert them into action by making the product, or imagining themselves making it in their mind. They need to feel the movements in their muscles as they imagine.

If the activities are auditory, they need to enact the descriptions with their body, or feel themselves doing it in their mind.

If there are tactile activities, they need to do them in larger size so as to involve their whole body. They can make drawings life-size on a large paper or board and make their sculptures larger. If constructing models, they can make them in true-to-life form. They can learn to ask questions to better understand the sequence of steps.

Activity: Converting Visual, Auditory, or Tactile Activities to Sequential Movement: Take a learning activity from any of the learner's school work that are visual, auditory, or tactile and have him or her convert it into action that is sequential. If getting up and physically moving is not possible in the situation, have him or her imagine himself acting out the movements mentally. The learner must actually feel the movements in his or her body while imagining the action.

Activity: Converting Information from Real-life Experiences for the Kinesthetic Left-brain Learner: Real-life experiences that have sequential instructions are best for kinesthetic left-brain people. They learn best on the spot. Apprenticeships in real life work situations provide the activity level they need to match the way they learn best. If instead of learning in a classroom with mostly visual and auditory modes of instruction, they are apprenticed to people who actually work in the field, they learn best.

If the training is mostly visual or auditory, they can role-play themselves doing the task, or imagine and experience their body doing the task in their mind. If the training is tactile, they can physically try to act out the steps, or make the product in larger size.

If the instruction is not step-by-step, they need to learn to ask questions so they can get the sequence right. If needed, they can jot down some notes on flip chart paper, a white board, or poster paper while standing up, using action words to specify what they should do.

It has been traditional that vocational courses provide real-life experiences such as driver's education, wood shop, cooking, auto repair, agriculture, etc. However, all courses, even in the more academic subjects can be made experiential as well. Why do science courses have to be mostly textbook based? Textbooks are important for reading about the research of others that came before. But along with that, why can't trainees or students apprentice in a biology lab, hospital, medical research lab, space center, Fermi lab, or other place where trained scientists work? Why do math students have to sit in a classroom doing textbook assignments when they can apprentice with accountants, stockbrokers, tax brokers, bankers, financial planners, or computer engineers? Why couldn't trainees or students in English courses, while learning the skills, also work in a publishing house, advertising company, newspaper, or research company? Kinesthetic people could do well in any subject if there is action and movement. We have limited their choices by making certain courses textbook (visual) based or lecture (auditory based). If every subject field offered real life experiences during the training, kinesthetic left-brain people would find themselves excelling in many more areas than those to which society has limited them.

Activity: Converting Information from Learning from a Person for the Kinesthetic Left-brain Learner: Why do so many kinesthetic left-brain people seem to do well in the courses that are vocational or athletic? Did anyone think through the kind of people who teach those courses? Think of coaches. Think of instructors in a wood shop or machine repair shop. How do they teach? Mostly kinesthetic (movement oriented) left-brain (able to give step-by-step directions). It is not the subject, but the person's method of teaching it that helps the material get through to other kinesthetic left-brain people. Why? Because a teacher who teaches kinesthetically and in a left-brain manner sets up activities that engage them in the way kinesthetic left-brain learners learn best. Imagine if athletes were forced to sit in a classroom and read a textbook and take written tests about their sports for several years and never have a chance to play. Imagine if the car mechanic read textbooks without having any hands-on experience to fix a car. We would find they would struggle as much with a textbook approach to action-oriented subjects as they do in many other academic courses. Kinesthetic left-brain people learn best when the person teaches in a kinesthetic left-brain way, coaching them through the action in a step-by-step way.

If they have to learn from a visual person, they should imagine themselves doing the action in their mind. They should convert the picture into three-dimensional action. They can also jot down the key action words in order of the steps while standing up or stretching out.

If they have to learn from an auditory person, see if that person can give them the directions. They should pay attention to the action words, and then act it out or imagine the action in their mind. If they want to remember, they can jot down some notes using action words, while standing up at a flip chart or white board.

If they are learning from a tactile person, they can get up and do the activity standing up, make the product on a white board or poster, or build a larger model so their muscles can be involved.

If the instructor in any of these modalities is too global, kinesthetic left-brain learners could ask questions to pin down the steps. If he or she still does not answer their questions, kinesthetic left-brain learners can make their own large-scale diagram of the steps as they perceive it. Then, they can check with someone else to help fill in any gaps in their understanding of the steps. If they need an outside resource, they can get hold of a video that shows them how to do the process.

They need to find as many ways as possible to keep themselves moving in a way that relates to the activity no matter in what situation they find themselves. In this way, they will not have to move in a nonproductive, uncooperative way. They can move in a way that fits the task and will find their attention will stay in whatever they are doing because they enjoy being successful in learning.

Personal Worksheet

Activity: List coping strategies from this chapter that you plan on using with the learner to convert material taught through other Superlinks styles into their own kinesthetic left-brain style.

Activities to Try

Strategy: Examples of Teaching Reading Skills to a Kinesthetic Left-brain Learner

Here are more examples to show how reading skills can be taught to kinesthetic left-brain learners: Included is an example of a phonics skill and a comprehension skill.

Strategy: Teaching a Phonics Skill in a Kinesthetic Left-brain Way:

Activity: Superlinks™ to Learning an Alphabet Letter:

Step 1: The child or teen should write the letter to be learned in large size in the air with the arm muscle of his or her writing hand while saying the letter and its sound.

Step 2: He or she should stand up and write the letter in large size on a flip chart, chalkboard, or dry-erase board on the wall. While writing the letter standing up, he or she should say the name of the letter and make the sound of it. For example, they should say, "D-- duh (the sound of the d) while writing.

Step 3: This should be repeated this five times.

Step 4: Reward the child for doing this by having him or her do a sports move like bounce a ball, throw a ring in ring toss, or jump rope.

When they learn phonics in their preferred Superlink™ style, by connecting the writing of the letter with their arm muscles, with their visual sense of seeing it, and the auditory sense of saying and hearing the sound, learning is accelerated, easier, and more fun because kinesthetic left-brain learners are working in the way they learn best.

Strategy: Teaching a Comprehension Skill in a Kinesthetic Left-brain Way:

Activity: Superlink™ to Time Order or Sequence in a Passage:

Step 1: Select a fiction story from the learner's schoolwork or from something they are reading for fun.

Step 2: Have him or her make large tag board cards for each event of the story.

Step 3: Mix up the tag board so the events are out of order.

Step 4: Have the learner put the tag board events back in time order by hanging the tag board with each event on a wall or poster board. Alternatively, they can lay the tag boards with the different events on the floor in time order. They can jump on the event in order after it is laid out on the floor.

Activity: Kinesthetic Drawing the Time Order: Another technique is that the learner can write the events from a story in time order of how they happened in large size on a flipchart or chalkboard using large motor muscles.

Activity: Time Order Building: Have the learner pretend to build any of the following: a piece of machinery, a vehicle, a house, a piece of furniture, a spaceship, a jet, a ship, or anything else they can think of. Constructing it requires putting the parts together in a

certain sequence. Have him or her get written directions for the task selected and build following the directions.
Activity: Cut Apart Project: Take the directions for a task that needs to be built. Cut the directions up so that each task is on a separate piece of tag board without having the learner see the original order of the directions. Mix them up. Have him or her figure out how to put them back in order, as they try to build it. They need to decide which steps need to be taken first, second, third, etc.
Activity: List the strategies in this chapter that you plan to use with the learner.

Activity to Try

Strategy: Kinesthetic Left-brain Superlinks™ Memory Technique:
Activity: Word Recall: In school, one has to remember different types of information. In science, one may be required to learn the different elements. In social studies, one may need to learn important historical dates and events. In literature, one may need to memorize quotations spoken by characters in a novel.

Here is an example activity to help a kinesthetic left-brain learner remember a list of words. The learner can apply this technique to remember material in any school subject!
Example word list: dog, house, rock, orange, baseball
Step 1: Tell the kinesthetic left-brain learner to imagine acting out a story with each word. Have him or her feel his or her muscles going through the motions associated with each word. The kinesthetic left-brain learner will connect the words in order. Say to the learner:

1) Pretend you are a dog and imagine yourself running.
2) Imagine yourself playing soccer outside your house.

3) Imagine yourself building something with large rocks. Feel your muscles lifting heavy rocks.
4) Imagine yourself picking oranges from an orange tree.
5) Imagine yourself hitting a baseball and getting a homerun.

Step 2: Ask the learner to repeat the five words in order reliving the stories he or she mentally imagined!

Personal Worksheet

Activity: List the memory strategies from this chapter that you plan on using with the learner to remember material presented through other Superlinks™ styles into his or her own kinesthetic left-brain style.

How a Kinesthetic Left-brain Learner Can Learn Anything Quickly

For the past thirty-nine years I have been teaching people of all ages how to learn any subject quickly. Kinesthetic left-brain learners can also learn anything quickly. Here are some strategies to help a kinesthetic left-brain learner convert any subject delivered in his or her non-preferred Superlink style and convert it into his or her preferred Superlink learning style.

How to Convert Input Delivered in Other Learning Styles into the Kinesthetic Left-brain Learners' Style

As the instructor, you now have some understanding of the way instruction can be delivered so that a kinesthetic right-brain learner can accelerate learning. You know the medium in which the material should be conveyed, the best materials, and the best environment for learning. So far so good. If you are the parent, you could help the teacher or educator teach in the way that will help your child or teen learn quickly. However, we do not always have control over the different factors. We may not be the ones in charge of getting the information conveyed through the best medium. We cannot always be in control of choosing the material. The learning environment is not always in our control. Is it hopeless? No, not at all. What you *can* do is convert any input into your child's best style. Your child can still learn, even if the medium, material, and environment does not suit his or her preferred Superlink style if they are converted. The following are coping skills to help convert any input into your child's or teen's own Superlink style. Think of it as a translation system.

Let us suppose the instructor or trainer does not convey information in the medium that is best for your child and has selected materials that does not match his or her Superlinks™ style. Further, let us suppose that the learning environment is not compatible with your child's best style. Here is what you can do to turn a poor situation into an optimal one.

Activity: Converting the Medium and Materials into The Learner's Kinesthetic Left-brain Superlink™

Directions: In the following list, the learner's best Superlink™ is listed on the left side. Across the top are listed the different media in which information is conveyed. Where the two intersect, you will find an asterisk (*) indicating that that is the correct media for the learner to use. If it is not the correct media, instructions on how to convert it into his or her best media is given.

Converting Printed Written Material for a Kinesthetic Left-Brain Learner

Activity

<u>Printed Written Material</u>

Conversion: The learner needs to act out the words or visualize the action in his or her mind in a step by step way and put into words.

Printed Graphic Material

Conversion: The learner needs to physically act out the graphic representation or visualize the action in his or her mind in a step by step way and put it into words.

Audio-Visual Material

Activity: Ideal for watching action on video, movies, television or animations and visualizing themselves doing the action and put into words.

Conversion: Slides, filmstrips need to be dramatized or action needs to be visualized sequentially and put into words.

Computers

Activity: Ideal for high-action computer programs with step by step directions that are interactive; interactive electronic communication networks that are interactive; virtual reality with step by step directions.

Conversion: Written text or graphics on computers need to be acted out or action visualized in the mind in a step by step way and put into words.

Activities

Activity: Ideal for activities involving movement in a step by step way and talking about it.

Conversion: Visual, auditory, and tactile activities need to be acted out or action visualized in the mind in a step by step way and put into words.

Real-Life Experience

Activity: Ideal for real-life experiences involving movement in a step by step way and put into words.

Conversion: Visual, auditory and tactile real-life experiences need to be acted out or action visualized in the mind in a step by step way and put into words.

Learning from a Person

Activity: Ideal if instructor provides movement activities in a step by step way with verbal directions.
Conversion: For visual, auditory and tactile instructors, need to act out or visualize action in the mind in a step by step way and put into words.

More Resources for Kinesthetic Left-brain Learners

To find out how to apply the learner's particular Superlink to learning anything quickly, select the topic you need from the list below to move on to other books, materials, trainings, and courses in our series for kinesthetic learners. These skills can help improve reading, memory, and learning in any content area whether science, social science, health, literature, health, a language, or any academic or vocational topic that involves reading or studying. Mastering kinesthetic reading will be an asset to learning any subject:
Activity: Think about which of the following skills will help the learner learn and be successful in the shortest possible time in any of the fields. You can select which strategies he or she needs, and continue their progress. Select the topic you need from the list below to move on to the other books, materials, trainings, and courses in our series for "Kinesthetic Learners." These skills can help improve reading, memory, and learning in any content area whether science, social science, health, literature, health, a language, or any academic or vocational topic that involves reading or studying.

Other Books and Resources by the Author, Ricki Linksman

(Books, eBooks, and Software, on the Brain; Memory Improvement; Accelerated Learning through Learning Styles and Brain Styles; Kinesthetic, Tactile, Visual, Auditory Left and Right Brain Learners; Reading and Listening Comprehension Strategies; Accelerated

Phonics; Vocabulary; Test-taking, Note-taking, and Study Skills and Test Prep for High School and College Entrance Exams, (ACT, SAT); Self-Esteem; Motivation; Concentration; and Focus
by Ricki Linksman)

How to Learn Anything Quickly: Quick, Easy Tips to Improve Memory, Reading Comprehension, Test-Taking Skills, and Learning through the Brain's Fastest Superlinks Learning Style

How to Improve Memory Quickly: Quick, Easy Tips to Improve Memory through the Brain's Fastest Superlinks Learning Style

The Fine Line between ADHD and Kinesthetic Learners: 197 Kinesthetic Activities to Quickly Improve Reading, Memory, and Learning in Just 10 Weeks: The Ultimate Parent Guide to ADD, ADHD, and Kinesthetic Learners

How to Improve Reading Comprehension Quickly by Knowing Your Personal Reading Comprehension Style: Quick, Easy Tips to Improve Comprehension through the Brain's Fastest Superlinks Learning Style

Solving Your Child's Reading Problem

From ADHD or ADD to A's: Improve Reading, Memory, and Learning Quickly for Kinesthetic Learners

The Power of Mental Golf, co-authored by Kerry Graham, LPGA Hall of Fame, Teaching and Club Professional Division and former president of LPGA, and Ricki Linksman

Your Child Can Be a Great Reader

Keys to Reading Success™: Internet Reading Program

Superlinks to Accelerated Learning Assessment™ (includes Linksman Learning Style Preference Assessment™ and Linksman Brain Hemispheric Preference Assessment™)

Off the Wall Phonics (Accelerated K-12, College, and Adult Phonics Program to Improve Reading Comprehension, Word Reading and Fluency for Kinesthetic, Tactile, Visual, and Auditory Learners, both Right-Brain and Left-Brain Learners)

Kinesthetic Vocabulary Activities Your Child Will Love

Tactile Vocabulary Activities Your Child Will Love

How to Quickly Improve Memory and Learning for Kinesthetic Left and Right Brain Superlinks Learning Styles

How to Quickly Improve Memory and Learning for Tactile Left and Right Brain Superlinks Learning Styles

How to Quickly Improve Memory and Learning for Visual Left and Right Brain Superlinks Learning Styles

How to Quickly Improve Memory and Learning for Auditory Left and Right Brain Superlinks Learning Styles

How to Quickly Improve Reading Comprehension for Kinesthetic Left and Right Brain Superlinks Learning Styles

How to Quickly Improve Reading Comprehension for Tactile Left and Right Brain Superlinks Learning Styles

How to Quickly Improve Reading Comprehension for Visual Left and Right Brain Superlinks Learning Styles

How to Quickly Improve Reading Comprehension for Auditory Left and Right Brain Superlinks Learning Styles

How to Quickly Improve Study, Note-taking and Test-taking Skills for Kinesthetic Left and Right Brain Superlinks Learning Styles

How to Quickly Improve Study, Note-taking and Test-taking Skills for Tactile Left and Right Brain Superlinks Learning Styles

How to Quickly Improve Study, Note-taking and Test-taking Skills for Visual Left and Right Brain Superlinks Learning Styles

How to Quickly Improve Study, Note-taking and Test-taking Skills for Auditory Left and Right Brain Superlinks Learning Styles

Vowel and Consonant Guide

Superlinks to Accelerated Learning: Phonics Diagnostic Test

For other products, books, eBooks, software, trainings, and e-courses visit:

www.readinginstruction.com
www.keyslearning.com
www.superlinkslearning.com
or e-mail: info@keyslearning.com

Kinesthetic left-brain learners can learn how to apply their kinesthetic left-brain learning techniques to be the best in any subject they want to master!

By using these methods, the kinesthetic learner will see a dramatic difference in reading and learning any subject rapidly and improving memory. May these methods propel any kinesthetic left-brain learner to success!

CONCLUSION

For students with ADHD or ADD or those who exhibit characteristics of ADHD or ADD but are merely kinesthetic learners, these techniques have taken them to be top students with "A"s in school.

It is my hope that you try these interventions with your student, child, teen or any adult learner to see them go from ADHD or ADD to A's!

APPENDIX

Sample Applications of Using the Learner's Superlinks to Learn Different Fields of Learning

As one embarks on a lifelong learning plan, one may encounter a variety of fields that one must learn. This section provides sample applications of how to use the learner's Kinesthetic Right-brain or Kinesthetic Left-brain Superlink to master different fields of learning. These samples provide examples to help he or she apply what they learned about their Superlink to accelerate learning to master different subjects.

The sample applications are in the following fields: math, writing, technical reading (computer manuals), the sciences, sports, and vocational fields and hobbies. For each subject, adaptations for each Superlink are provided giving the strategy to use to accelerate learning in that field.

Activity: Application of the Kinesthetic Right-brain and Left-brain Superlinks to Learning Math

Math is used in all segments of society. It is for business, for home and personal use, for school and college courses in math, or use of math in other fields such as science, economics, history, computer science, health, nutrition, art, music, or vocational fields. We can use our Superlink to accelerate our learning in the field of math. The following are some basic adaptations to use for learning any field of math using the Kinesthetic Right-brain or Kinesthetic Left-brain Superlink.

Kinesthetic Left-brain:

Activity: Physically act out a story problem using concrete real-life examples in a game, simulation, or role-play in a step-by-step way and talk about it. Write the numbers in large size while standing up at a board or flipchart, and talk through the problem in a step-by-step way. Use sports or game equipment or physical exercise or movement as a bonus for working out each problem to keep actively engaged while doing the math.

Kinesthetic Right-brain:

Activity: Physically act out the story problem with concrete, real-life examples in a global way with the answer. Do several examples of the same type of problem with the answers so the right side of the brain can understand the pattern of how to do it. Use large manipulatives to illustrate the problem. Write the numbers and the problem in large-size while standing up at a board or flipchart. Play sports, games, or do a physical activity while practicing the math problem. Keep the body physically.

Activity: Application of Kinesthetic Right-brain and Left-brain Superlinks to Learn the Sciences

While each discipline has its own tradition, any subject can be adapted to be compatible with each of the Superlinks. There are many fields of sciences, but there are certain common characteristics in learning each of them: reading research of others, and experimenting by forming hypotheses and testing them using the scientific method. These processes can be adapted for the Kinesthetic Right-brain Learner and Kinesthetic Left-brain Learner so that anyone of any Superlink can be successful in the sciences.

Kinesthetic Left-brain:

Activity: As the learner reads scientific material, they need to visualize themselves sequentially doing the actions described. If possible, physically perform the actions described in the reading in a step-by-step way as they read. Read while working on the actual science equipment. Plan his or her experiment by making a large left-brain outline on a flipchart or board as he or she reads, while standing up. Talk through the steps aloud as he or she performs them. Wherever possible, relate the material to the actual performance of the task. The learner need to keep a record of what he or she has done by making a large chart on a board while standing up. They will do well to work in a group setting, making it more active and lively.

Kinesthetic Right-brain:

Activity: Have the learner look over the material, focusing on the introduction and the conclusion and the main headings before reading. They need to look at any diagrams, pictures, or charts first. As he or she goes through the science readings, they need to make a large size mind map on a flip chart or large board while standing up, sketching out with pictures and key words the main points. Have them draw or sketch out while standing up his or her plan for the experiment. Use color, symbols, and icons wherever possible. Do the experiment and record the results in a mind map on a flipchart, with sketches. He or she will probably want to jump right in and do it, and learn by trial and error. They can do so, but double check to make sure they are working in the right direction. He or she will do well to work in a group setting, making it more active and lively.

Activity: Application of Kinesthetic Right-brain and Left-brain Superlinks to Learn a Sport or Dance

Some people seem to take naturally to sports or dance. They just seem to pick these up with natural ease. Sports and dance are other areas that can be best learned if adapted to one's natural style of learning. People of all Superlinks can master sports or dance if instruction is compatible with the way their brain thinks. The following are adaptations so that kinesthetic right-brain

or left-brain learners or can master sports and dance.
Kinesthetic Left-brain:
Activity: Join in with others who are performing the sport or dance and follow along in a step-by-step way. The instructor will guide the learner through it, giving him or her step-by-step verbal directions and they will carry it out as they listen. His or her kinesthetic sense will get an automatic feel for the movements and it will come easily and naturally for them. He or she can pick it up just by working with others who are performing it in a step-by-step way.
Kinesthetic Right-brain:
Activity: The kinesthetic right-brain learner will learn it by just jumping in and doing the sport or dance with others. They need to observe the entire process first so they have the big picture or overview. Then he or she just needs to get involved by doing it. Learning a sport or dance by doing it comes easily for them. By participating, they learn by trial and error. A coach can guide him or her where they need refinement. The action and movement of the sports and dance, and fun of competition makes this an easy area for them to master.

Activity: Application of Superlinks for Kinesthetic Right-brain or Kinesthetic Left-brain Learners to Learn Vocational Fields and Hobbies

There are numerous vocational fields and hobbies in which people are engaged for work and play. These involve learning a skill that needs to be performed. This area ranges encompasses construction, architecture, designing, landscaping, interior decoration, plumbing, electrical engineering, painting, wallpapering, gardening, agriculture, farming, carpentry, building airplanes, trucks, or cars, delivery, driving, trucking, shipping, sales, marketing, crafts, textiles, sewing, knitting, fashion designing, jewelry making, modeling, art, music, machine repairs, restaurant and food industry, entertainment, and numerous other fields. Learning any of these fields can become easy and quicker if the instruction is adapted to our Superlink. The following are adaptations to help Kinesthetic Right-brain and Kinesthetic Left-brain Learners accelerate learning of these fields through his or her preferred Superlink.

Kinesthetic Left-brain:

Activity: The learner will join in with others who are performing the task and follow along in a step-by-step way. The instructor will guide him or her through it, giving them step-by-step verbal directions and he or she will carry it out as they listen. His or her kinesthetic sense will get an automatic feel for the job and it will come easily and naturally for them. He or she can pick it up just by working with others who are performing it in a step-by-step way.

Kinesthetic Right-brain:

Activity: The kinesthetic right-brain learner will learn it by just jumping in and doing the task with others. He or she needs to observe the entire process first so they have the big picture or overview. He or she needs to just get involved by doing it. Learning by doing comes easily for them. By participating, he or she learns by trial and error. The instructor will guide the learner where they need refinement. The action and movement of a skill or task makes this easy for them to learn.

About the Author: Ricki Linksman

Ricki Linksman is the author and developer of one of the fastest brain-based memory improvement, accelerated learning, learn to read, improve reading comprehension, and learn anything quickly program in the world today. She is the author of many books, including *How to Learn Anything Quickly: Quick, Easy Tips to Improve Memory, Reading, Comprehension, Test-Taking, and Learning through the Brain's Fastest Superlinks Learning Style (*previously published by Barnes and Noble*)*; *The Fine Line between ADHD and Kinesthetic Learners: 197 Kinesthetic Activities to Quickly Improve Reading, Memory, and Learning in Just 10 Weeks: The Ultimate Parent Handbook for ADHD, ADD, and Kinesthetic Learners*; *How to Improve Memory Quickly by Knowing Your Personal Memory Style: Quick, Easy Tips to Improve Memory through the Brain's Fastest Superlinks Memory and Learning Style*; *Your Child Can Be a Great Reader*; and *Solving Your Child's Reading Problems*, featured *in Publisher's Weekly, Women's World, Family Life, Chicago Parent, Chicago Tribune, Los Angeles Parent, San Diego Parent*, the *Naperville Sun*, and the *Lisle Sun*. She has written numerous other books on accelerated learning and reading comprehension. Her newest one is *The Power of Mental Golf,* co-authored by Kerry R. Graham, LPGA Hall of Fame, Teaching and Club Professional Division and former president of LPGA, and Ricki Linksman, where Superlinks learning and brain styles can be used by golfers, golf professionals, and golf instructors and coaches to dramatically improve golf instruction and accelerate the speed of learning golf through a golfer's best way of learning.

Ricki Linksman is the founder-director of National Reading Diagnostics Institute, headquartered in

Naperville, Illinois, near Chicago, a training institution to help people of all ages accelerate learning and improve their memory through Superlinks™ a system she developed using neuroscience and brain research, learning styles, and brain styles. Through Ricki Linksman's methods, people can improve their performance on their job and in their studies. By improving comprehension and memory of what they read, people can excel in any field. She runs a training institution in which trainers, sports and life coaches, instructors, administrators, employers, and teachers in any field can learn how to be more effective in training employees, students, and trainees.

She also directs a parent center in which she offers reading diagnostic testing and learning style and brain style inventory assessments to find one's fastest way of learning and remembering. Through diagnostic testing her methods include developing an individual prescriptive plan followed by coaching, teaching, and tutoring students from pre-K, kindergarten, Grades 1 through Grades 12, college, to adult learners. Students show dramatic improvement whether they are in regular education, special education, Title 1, remedial reading, have ADHD or ADD, are in bilingual or ESOL, ELL, ESL, or dual language programs, or who are gifted. She was the developer of one of the first parent involvement programs in the country, and was featured in Cendant and Davidson's Reading Blaster™ 9-12 popular software program as creating a "Parent Tips" guidebook, and has chosen as one of the best reading experts in the country to consult in the production of Cendant's *Learn to Read*™ software package.

At National Reading Diagnostics Institute, parents are trained how to accelerate their children's or teens' memory and learning. Her Keys to Reading Success™ program includes parent involvement worksheets to help parents be more effective in providing homework help.

Ricki has been serving students in public and private schools throughout the country and around the world. Whenever she has set up the system of accelerated learning and accelerated reading in schools, those schools have raised test scores and achievement through her memory methods within less than one school year. Test scores raised include CTBS, SAT, ACT, and ISAT (Illinois State Achievement Test). Her memory improvement program has also been used to prepare students for career examinations in diverse fields, such as medicine and law.

Ricki Linksman is also the developer of *Keys to Reading Success*™ an Internet-based pre-K, kindergarten, grades 1 through 12, and college reading program to use accelerated learning and memory techniques and learning styles and brain hemispheric preference strategies to teach students to learn to read or improve reading within four to eight months or less. The average success rate is 98-99% of all K-12 students using the program rise 2-5 grade levels in reading in 6-8 months, including students in regular education, special education, ELL, ESL, ESOL, bi-lingual and dual language, Title 1 or Remedial Reading, and gifted programs (and those with ADD or ADHD). Rusty Acree, a retired veteran and current football referee, of Richmond, Virginia, is one of many parents and grandparents who have seen the effectiveness of the program on his grandson. His grandson, who had been previously labeled with ADHD, had been left back in kindergarten for two years, yet still could neither recognize the letters of the alphabet nor read a word. When he was diagnosed by Ricki as a kinesthetic right-brain learner and was taught how to read through his kinesthetic right-brain Superlinks style he was able to learn the letters of the alphabet and could read his first book ever within 2 days. Rusty Acree who continued to see the phenomenal growth of his grandson over the next year to get to grade level in reading has called Ricki Linksman, "The Michael Jordan of Reading."

Ricki developed the *Superlinks to Accelerated Learning*™ program with its *Linksman Learning Style Preference Assessment and Brain Hemispheric Preference Assessment*™ used to discover a person's best memory Superlink (learning style and brain style) to accelerate learning.

Her programs Keys to Reading Success™ and Superlinks to Accelerated Learning™ were selected by a foundation, the "Cotchery Foundation," started by New York Jets football running back, Jericho Cotchery and his wife Mercedes Cotchery, to assist an elementary school in North Carolina raise its reading scores and is featured on the Cotchery Foundation website.

Her award-winning phonics program has been selected for use as the phonics curriculum used by Huntington™ Learning Centers throughout the country. Other companies that have used her Superlinks to Accelerated Learning™ programs include Kaplan On-line University; MFS Investment Management, Boston, a large Massachusetts financial institution who used Ricki Linksman's accelerated learning techniques to help trainers teach clients about mutual funds sales; and by one of the largest technology company in the world.

Ricki Linksman created a phonics program specially designed for kinesthetic and tactile learners, but can be used with visual and auditory learners also, including those with a right-brain or left-brain preference, called Off the Wall Phonics™. It allows students to learn to master and remember every phonics patterns in the English language to move someone from beginning reading to college-level word reading ability within 10 game levels, of 10 games each. If followed, any student can raise their word-reading level, which can help their reading comprehension, by playing one game level per week for ten weeks, and studies have proven the average raise in word-reading level to be two to five grade levels in reading in that time.

A university football team used Keys to Reading Success™ and Superlinks to Accelerated Learning™ to improve football performance through learning and memory styles and brain styles, helping them to their first winning season. It dramatically changed the way football coaches taught the football play book to the athletes.

She has worked as a consultant to golf instructors to improve teaching of golf through Superlinks to Accelerated Learning™ learning styles. She was a consultant to a former White Sox baseball player on product development of a pitching aid to improve pitching skills using Superlinks to Accelerated Learning™ As a trainer of trainers she has improved the effectiveness of trainers to help them reach all participants of different learning styles.

Four schools and educational institutions in South Africa from elementary school to a college, including Learning Identity, Clifton Preparatory School, and Hilton College, have adopted Keys to Reading Success and Superlinks to Accelerated Learning to improve memory and reading.

Ricki works as a consultant to businesses, companies, and educational institutions to help people accelerate and improve memory and learning in any field. She has done trainings for college professors and instructors at colleges and universities. She has also done volunteer work training tutors for Literacy Volunteers for America. She trained facilitators for youth outreach programs sponsored by a local police station and worked with students from DCFS (Department of Children and Family Services). She has also served as a reading expert for a pro-bono court case for a major Chicago law firm. Public schools call on Ricki Linksman's expertise on case study teams for students.

She has run Administrator Academies in Illinois on District Reading Improvement, training superintendents and principals in steps to improve their district reading programs and scores. She has been one of the trainers for Illinois's ISAT (Illinois State Achievement Test) reading and writing tests and has trained teachers in how to raise test scores on this state test. She was one of Illinois's state validators for the Right to Reading Initiative. She has presented memory and learning strategies to many Regional Offices of Education to train teachers and administrators from many school districts in these methods.

She gives seminars and workshops, appears at book-signings, and speaks at conferences. She has presented her memory improvement and reading programs to tens of thousands of teachers across the country. She works as a consultant and trainer for public school districts and schools in accelerated learning techniques, raising district reading scores, and improving student achievement. She received a certificate of merit from the IASCD (Illinois Association for Supervision and Curriculum) 1999 Winn's Research Award for "Maximizing School Reading Scores."

She receives thousands of letters and emails from teachers, administrators, parents, college professors, consultants, and students from all over the world who have read her books and write to her for advice on improving memory, reading, and learning performance. Her works are cited on numerous Internet sites listing excellent resources for parents and teachers, including *Conde Nast*.

She has taught graduate education courses in reading, and another on inclusion: differentiated learning to teach to all learners through learning styles. Specializing in accelerated learning and memory improvement with application to reading, she has taught these techniques to students of all ages and to adults.

For parents and teachers, she has numerous books, EBooks, courses, online e-courses, podcasts, webinars, teleseminars, coaching, and consulting to accelerate learning for all types of learners, including kinesthetic, tactile, auditory, visual, with either a right-brain or left-brain preference. These materials have helped children and teens from pre-K, kindergarten, grade 1-12, and college, whether in regular education, special education, gifted, ESOL, ELL, ESL, bi-lingual or dual language, or Title 1 or Reading Remedial programs, or those who have ADHD or ADD.

Contact Information:
Ricki Linksman can be contacted at: National Reading Diagnostics Institute and Keys Learning, Naperville, Illinois;
Email: info@keyslearning.com
Web sites:

http://www.readinginstruction.com
http://www.keyslearning.com
http://www.keystoreadingsuccess.com
http://www.superlinkslearning.com
http://www.nationalreadingdiagnosticsinstitute.co
m
http://www.offthewallphonics.com

A Special Gift for Readers

The author has a special gift for readers of this book, *How to Improve Memory Quickly by Knowing Your Personal Memory Style: Quick, Easy Tips to Improve Memory through the Brain's Fastest Superlinks Memory and Learning Style*. If you would like to find your Superlinks memory and learning style and brain hemispheric preference style, or that of your family, friends, and others, as a special reader of *How to Improve Memory Quickly by Knowing Your Personal Memory Style: Quick, Easy Tips to Improve Memory through the Brain's Fastest Superlinks Memory and Learning Style*, here is your special discount code to access the test at a significant discount. Go to: http://www.readinginstructiom.com and from the Explore Learning Store, select Superlinks to Accelerated Learning™ Assessment and enter the discount code: HTLAQ

Note: When you get to the check-out page, scroll down to enter your discount code and the discounted price will appear at check-out. After taking the test, it will instantly be scored and give you a personalized report on your best memory Superlink learning style and brain style with tips on how to improve memory quickly. You can return to the matching chapter in this book to read about how you can improve memory quickly through your Superlinks memory and learning style and brain style and improve your own or others' memory. Enjoy the rewards of personal transformation!

For readers who enjoyed this book and feel it can help others, please visit amazon.com or other online sites if you want to write a review of how you enjoyed the book so that other struggling parents and teachers can help their child or students also go from pain and frustration to success.

Made in the USA
Las Vegas, NV
04 April 2022